OUT OF THE PULPIT
INTO THE PEW

OUT OF THE PULPIT INTO THE PEW

a pastor's guide to meaningful service after retirement

GENE WILLIAMS

BEACON HILL PRESS
OF KANSAS CITY

ISBN-13: 978-0-8341-2322-9
ISBN-10: 0-8341-2322-3

Cover Design: J.R. Caines
Interior Design: Sharon Page

Library of Congress Cataloging-in-Publication Data

Williams, Gene, 1932-
  Out of the pulpit, into the pew : a pastor's guide to meaningful service after retire-
ment / Gene Williams.
    p. cm.
  ISBN-13: 978-0-8341-2322-9 (pbk.)
  ISBN-10: 0-8341-2322-3 (pbk.)
  1. Clergy—Retirement. I. Title.

  BV4382.W55 2007
  253.086'96—dc22

                                                                    2007024259

10 9 8 7 6 5 4 3 2 1

CONTENTS

FOREWORD

This is a practical, wise, and God-honoring book from a man who has not only been there but *is* there. Retired? Not on his life. A changed ministry? Of course. Obstacles to overcome? Real ones, addressed candidly and realistically. *Out of the Pulpit, into the Pew* needs to be read by all serious Christians, pastors and laypersons as well, who want their golden years to be golden for God.

For 11 years, my wife, Rachael, and I lived in a retirement community in a warm, southern state with a golf course in every neighborhood. We were saddened as we observed the apathy of some Christians who were retired from good secular work and from the ministry. We saw men and women, a few pastors included, who had ministered in congregations "up north," who were living out an "eat, drink and be merry, for tomorrow we die" philosophy.

How sad. How lonely. How unnecessary. And worse, a departure from the divine design. Our God is a trinity of persons, a community. We are called to live in community, serving others, until we go home to enjoy forever the eternal relationships of perfect love.

Gene and I have never met. But Gene's wife, Joyce, and Rachael share a passion for ministry that advancing years cannot dim. Gene's book testifies to a life filled with fire that, with practical tips scattered on every page, can spark a similar passion in many others.

Rachael and I have had the privilege of being on the leadership team for a unique Sunday School class called The Symphony Class. Nearly 100 people of all ages, from 21 to 86, serve together like an orchestra with many instruments to make beautiful music together—truly a Christian symphony.

If you're nearing retirement age, if you're already there, or if you know people who are in their retirement years, read this book and pass it on. Gene clearly models and points the way for pastors and all Christians to enjoy a fulfilling, meaningful service that pleases God.

—Larry Crabb
Author, speaker, psychologist

INTRODUCTION

The age of 65 has long been the target date for retirement for most North Americans, including many ministers. No more hard work, long meetings, or exhausting obligations—finally burdens and commitments can be laid down while rest and pleasure take over. From that point on, the retiree can sleep late, play favorite games, or enjoy some favored pastime. It's vacation day every day!

Or is it? In an article by Julia Burton-Jones titled *Retirement: A Second Vocation,* she asks, "Do *you* feel you have a God-given right to retire at a certain age? If so, where does this sense of entitlement come from?"[1]

You may want to take a serious look at this "golden age." Most of our lives we have heard "the grass is always greener on the other side." From whatever side of the fence we are looking the distant fields appear beautiful. However, life's experiences teach us that once we get to that green field, we find there are some bare spots and ugly areas. And we can be sure this is true in ministerial retirement as well.

So, when the day comes and we reach that magic number—65—we may very well learn that it's not exactly the way we anticipated. After a few weeks of leisure and nothingness, boredom often sets in. Then we learn that financial arrangements that should have provided for all needs don't even come close. In some cases a mate's health deteriorates and the spouse becomes a full-time caregiver. The emotional stress of facing the questions "Who am I? Why am I here? What can I do for the Kingdom?" may be overwhelming.

Since the Bible does not set guidelines for prophetical retirement, we are left to our choices as to how we respond. Retirement can be a rich experience if we approach it with a healthy attitude and some well-laid plans. It doesn't have to be a time to start sitting on a shelf and gathering dust. It can be a very fruitful period when we give love service to God and experience the warmth of a deepened relationship with Him. As a result, we can strengthen our sense of purpose and self-worth.

I believe the army of retired ministers may be a vast, untapped resource for the Kingdom. While we can no longer carry the heavy loads we once shouldered, surely we can do *something*. We just need to find God's new assignments for us. We may very well be likened to an army of ants. While none of us can carry a huge load, by working together we can make a dramatic difference. The truth is—the Church needs us, and we need to be needed. Our involvement in the Kingdom can be a love service to God—and love service is always richly rewarding.

Maybe that's the key. What do I most enjoy doing? I'll never forget a phone call I received from Grace, a 75-year-old lady who was teaching a Sunday School class in the last church I pastored. She said, "Pastor, my nerves just will not let me keep teaching my children's class, but I want to do something. As you know, I'm a pretty good cook." Actually, she was a *great* cook. She went on to say, "If I can use that gift for God, I would be pleased to do so."

It didn't take long to come up with a visitation program that involved delivering some of her fresh-baked fruit pies to our first-time guests. I organized a special friendship team to work with Grace in order to utilize her baking talents. Grace burned up two ovens baking pies in her own kitchen. Before she quit, she had baked over 2,000 delicious fruit pies.

I still remember Grace's excitement the week pie number 2,000 came out of her oven. And she rejoiced at all the new members in our congregation whose first personal touch with our family of believers was the delivery of one of her delicious pies.

I'm also challenged by the attitude of my pastor friend Amos Williams. I remember visiting him when he was 84 years old and thinking he was so frail and weak he certainly did not have long to live. Wrong! Amos recovered, gained strength, and at 91 is breathing life into a congregation that was all but dead. The district superintendent was seriously considering closing the church. Amos asked to be given the opportunity to see what could be done with the remnant. There was nothing to lose, so the district superintendent said, "Give it a try." Smart move! Amos's attitude so excited the 5 remaining members that there are now over 40 people worshiping together each Sunday. He will not allow them to feel sorry for themselves. They have taken on financial responsibilities they had ignored for years. He is excited, and his attitude is infectious to his people. Amos always says in no uncertain terms that he is having fun, there is work to be done, and he is not about to quit.

Like these two retired "ants," I believe there is a vast army that should be available to the church. This number could really grow if better plans were laid for them to be able to serve rather than survive. Yes, there will come a day when health problems and other challenges simply will not allow us to serve, and we must accept this reality of life. However, until then there is no reason to sit on our hands and wait for the inevitable. Surely none of us feel that our "account of debt to God" has been paid in full.

There are some subjects that need to be addressed for our preparation to be adequate for a truly rewarding retirement.

- Take care of financial needs in advance. Start planning as early as possible with a definite financial plan.

- Discover your opportunities in the Kingdom in your new role in life. Such things as mentoring young pastors can be mutually rewarding. Teaching in a variety of venues can be beneficial, including assisting young pastors with their congregation's visitation needs. Identify clearly how you can support and encourage the pastor of the church you attend. Many a Moses needs an Aaron to help him carry the load that we once carried. For those of us who are Aarons, service to the Kingdom is not over; it has only been changed to a new assignment that is more compatible with our physical conditions.

- Learn to live with some health issues. This is a part of the aging process, and every retiree must learn to make the adaptations needed when health is no longer as vigorous as it once was. Also, it is important to learn to be a caregiver to a mate whose health has deteriorated.

- Discover ministering activities that provide deep satisfaction. There are many opportunities for ministering outside the local church—care homes, service projects in line with physical capabilities, and so forth.

- Discover how to keep life exciting. In order to maintain our sense of self-worth, we need to be involved in some productive activity.

Again, Julia Burton-Jones says, "If God ordained work as a source of human identity, lacking purposeful 'work' is by implication dehumanising. Work is intended as a means of channelling our energies and our God-given creative urge. If it is an integral part of what makes us human, how can we say that older people can do without it?"[2]

She then refers to Paul Tournier in his book *Learning to Grow Old:*

He looks at concepts of work and leisure and argues for a redefining of both. The term he uses to great effect is "vocation." He embraces leisure and the pursuit of hobbies as a valuable channelling of human energy throughout life, but he argues for retirement to be characterised also by a search for a new calling or vocation, a "second career." . . . I am reminded of many retired Christians I know who faithfully invest their time, skill and energy in voluntary and charitable activity. Without the dedication of these individuals, the voluntary sector would collapse.[3]

So if you are a member of the army of ants, life is not over. There is much yet to be done and enjoyed. Essentially, we need to prepare for retirement in a way that will let us continue to enjoy the rich rewards of ministry. In retirement, ministry continues to be a great source of joy for me. To be sure, my opportunity to serve Him has changed, but my will to serve has not weakened. Obviously, I loved being a pastor. I loved God's will for my life then, and I love it now.

So in retirement, ministry goes on. Muriel Larson wrote an article in *Retirement with a Purpose* titled "Retirement Without Trauma." She states, "Retirement may prove to be a traumatic experience. But for Christians it can be perhaps the most exciting and challenging time of their lives!"[4] While her message is primarily aimed at the larger lay Christian population, it can certainly be applied to retiring ministers.

She goes on to quote Isa. 58:11—"The Lord will guide you always; he will satisfy your needs"—and comments, "Retired Christians can be a blessing to all they meet. They know God will care for all their needs. They can glorify the Lord with their faith and testimony. Younger Christians can draw strength and encouragement from them. Their sunset years can be filled with rich experiences if they keep loving, trusting, and serving the Lord."[5]

May God help every minister who has or ever will retire hear that ringing promise, "Sunset years can be filled with rich experiences if [we] keep loving, trusting, and serving the Lord."

Whether or not that happens may very well depend on which way we are looking. In their wonderful book *How to*

Make the Rest of Your Life the Best of Your Life, Mark Victor Hansen and 94-year-old Art Linkletter state, "Backward or forward? That's your choice. You can choose to look backward and relive the past failures, injuries, and missed opportunities. Or you can choose to learn from the past and look ahead to the adventures and possibilities that lie in your future. Which you choose to do will have a great deal to do with whether you spend your Second Prime [your retired years] active, vigorous, and hopeful or bitter, angry, and frail."[6]

We retirees are in our second prime. So determine right now to make these years active, vigorous, and helpful for the kingdom of God. There are enough of us ants to make a significant difference if we will.

leaving the pulpit

1
CHANGE
HAPPENS!

Nothing stays the same forever. Sooner or later there will be major changes for everyone. In our younger years this fact rarely crosses our minds because we are getting stronger and wiser all the time. We like what's happening. Our bodies have not started to complain. We are on an upward journey that has no indication it will ever end.

But it does end!

We reach the top of our life's mountain—however high or low that might be. And from that point on, changes begin to happen. Our energy level is not what it once was. We feel pain in joints that we have always taken for granted. Life is just not quite like it was a few years ago.

I have always been blessed to be one of those high-energy, long-endurance, "I can do anything" people. I remember working all day and then getting into the car to drive all night. Energy was no problem. When it came to hard physical labor, my motto was "Count me in!"

Things have changed. Now I look at some physical activities, and my heart says, "I can do that!" only to hear my body say, "I don't think so!" If I insist on forcing the issue, I usually pay a high price. Bodies change, and we either learn to adjust or suffer the consequences. In their book *The New Retirement*, Jan Cullinane and Cathy Fitzgerald point out, "Obviously, retirement brings about a shift in roles and activity. Those who can adjust and adapt to these changes will have a more successful transition to retirement." They further emphasize, "Retirement is now recognized as a process involving perhaps several forays into and out of alternative projects, pastimes, and jobs. Newly retired persons may have different experiences than those who have been retired for longer periods."[1]

Change happens in every aspect of our lives. We must learn to make adjustments if we are going to make the most of what we have to work with. Sure, we can resist, live a rigid "I refuse to adjust" life if we choose. However, we need to know that every day we live will be different from the day before. Change is taking place. People who learn to adjust continue to enjoy life. Those who do not adjust slowly but surely become miserable. This is never more evident than in the lives of those of us who are in ministry.

Two years before I retired, one of my good friends gave me a copy of the contemporary book by Spencer Johnson *Who Moved My Cheese?* In case you haven't read it, my friend Wes Tracy presents an excellent summary of this best seller in his book *Younger than I Used to Be.*

This modern parable is about two mice, Sniff and Scurry, and two mouse-sized "little people" Hem and Haw. All four lived in a maze. Each day they venture out into the maze in search of cheese. For a long, long time they dined daily at Cheese Station C. They don't know where the cheese came from, but it's always there, plenty for all four.

But one day they arrive at Cheese Station C and discover that the cheese is gone. "Who moved my cheese?" Hem and Haw bellow in anguish. They rant about the injustice of it all. Their life depends on the cheese. They planned their future with cheese in mind.

Sniff and Scurry have discovered that the cheese is gone. Soon they are off into the maze to search for new cheese. Hem and Haw, however, are not ready for the change. They decide to think it over. They decide that since the cheese has always been there, it will return. So they wait—and get hungrier and weaker. One day Haw decides that he must search for new cheese. Hem won't go along with such nonsense. He says that the maze is dangerous. "I like it here. It's comfortable. It's what I know . . . I'm getting too old for that." He thinks that in searching for new cheese he'll get lost and make a fool of himself.

Haw leaves him behind and after searching many mazes he discovers Cheese Station N. It's the biggest mountain of cheese he's ever seen. In the story the "cheese" stands for whatever brings you meaning, purpose, and happiness. It represents what nourishes the soul and spirit. The cheese is what you build the core of your life around—your source of identity, contentment, and fulfillment.[2]

Many ministerial retirees need to find Cheese Station N but will have to accept the fact that a major change has taken place in their lives before they will ever make that discovery. That happened to me.

Change Came to Me

I loved my calling to pastoral ministry. In fact, I think I was addicted to it. As strange as it might sound, I even enjoyed middle-of-the-night calls to the hospitals. They meant I could minister at the point of need. I thrived on the activities around the church. I know some people won't understand how that could be, but that was my experience.

For 45 years, thoughts of retirement hardly crossed my mind. There were sermons to prepare and people to lead. At the age of 50 it did dawn on me that my wife and I would need a place to live. We were in a church-owned parsonage at that time. So we asked for and received a housing allowance and bought our own home. At least we had a roof (that we owned) over our heads. I participated in Social Security, my denomination provided a small pension, and my last church opened an individual retirement account for me. So, for me the physical and financial needs for retirement appeared to be under control. Why should I think about it anymore? Retirement was covered—if it ever happened at all.

How wrong I was! There was no way I was even close to being prepared for the changes that were coming my way. As I closed in on the magic age of 65, I was still in good health and had a high energy level. However, some of my people realized I was advancing in years and encouraged me to rest from my labors. My church was very generous and treated us to a wonderful retirement package.

I should have been ready to happily ride off into the sunset. I wasn't, and I didn't. I began to suffer some mild depression. Remember—I was addicted to ministry, and withdrawal did not happen smoothly. Questions haunted me: "Who am I? What is my assignment? I'm no longer a pastor, and I'm not an evangelist. But I must continue to serve God in some way. How? My account is not paid in full, and I know I'll always be deeply in debt. But I want to keep serving in some way." Frankly, I was not mentally or emotionally ready for the change that was taking place in my life.

My wife, Joyce, encouraged me to take hold of the promise in Hab. 1:5, "I am going to do something in your days that you would not believe even if you were told." She kept assuring me that we would see what God had planned for us.

When we stop being obstinate and resistant and let the Lord guide our transitions, He will help us make the adjustments necessary to go on making the most of our lives.

In His kindness, God opened the door for us to do some work with the Billy Graham Evangelistic Association. My second assignment was in Charlottesville, Virginia, teaching Christian Life and Witness classes for a crusade that was to take place there. While I was happy to have something to do, I still struggled over my calling. I had not been able to accept the changes taking place in my life.

As He always does, God helped this struggling servant. The last day of the month-long assignment in Charlottesville, I received a call from the crusade office. Bruce Pringle, counseling and follow-up director for the crusade, had gone home to Canada for a visit. Upon his return, he was delayed at the Canadian border. Consequently, he would not be able to teach his class that evening. Bruce called the office and told them to have me teach it. When the call came I resisted, because I was scheduled at another location. However, upon being reminded that Bruce was in charge, I agreed to change. (There's that magic word.)

The class that evening was the first time I met with that particular group. It was the final night of four weeks of training. About 230 were present. When I was introduced, the word *pastor* was not used, and no one but Joyce was aware of my struggles.

Just as I began teaching, a young Korean lady seated on

the third pew began to weep. Frankly, I thought that was strange since I had not shared any sad stories or anything else to elicit such an emotional response. I was curious, but I had a class to teach. So I overlooked her response and went on with the lesson.

When the class was over I went to a table to sign up crusade counselors. This young lady, named Connie, went to Joyce and said, "I have a message from God for Pastor."

Joyce responded, "Excuse me?"

Connie repeated, "I have a message from God for Pastor."

Being protective of my fragile emotions, Joyce said, "Maybe you had better tell me."

Connie very calmly stated, "I've been studying 2 Corinthians. God gave a message to me to deliver to someone. When I asked Him who the message was for, He said, 'I'll tell you when it's time.' When Pastor stood up to teach, God whispered to me, 'That is the man who needs your message.'" She then read 2 Cor. 5:17-20 from her Bible:

> If anyone is in Christ, he is a new creation; the old has gone, the new has come! All this is from God, who reconciled us to himself through Christ and gave us the ministry of reconciliation: that God was reconciling the world to himself in Christ, not counting men's sins against them. And he has committed to us the message of reconciliation. *We are therefore Christ's ambassadors, as though God were making his appeal through us* (emphasis added).

Then Connie uttered the words that helped change my attitude toward retirement. She said, "God wants Pastor to know that his ministry is not over. He needs to know that he is an ambassador under special assignment." Joyce replied, "You must go tell my husband." Connie did, and my life was turned around.

Ministry wasn't over—it had just taken on a different look. Since I accepted the change, all depression is gone. No, I'm no longer pastor to a local congregation. God has given a different assignment to me. In my case it became much broader than I ever would have dreamed. Habakkuk 1:5 has been proven true. I would have continued to struggle with the idea if He had not revealed His plan to me in such a special way.

The Call

I believe God wants all of His ministers to be under special assignment. Some will be pastors, others teachers or evangelists. But each one of us has something we can do. Why should we sit on a shelf and gather dust when we can be ambassadors? Frankly, at the ripe age of 75 I'm still having fun serving God. Yes, I play a little more golf and fish more than I once did, but I find it richly rewarding to still be in His army.

If this change has come to you, make the most of it. As an army of ants, we're an exclusive club. A person must be retired to enlist in this army, but when we enlist we need to get ready for some wonderful experiences.

If you're one of those for whom retirement is in the future, make plans now so you can enjoy this wonderful time in your life. To paraphrase Martin Seligman, who studied happiness and optimism for over 25 years, it is important to find your calling. You can find employment and earn a paycheck, perhaps power, or maybe even prestige, but a calling will bring a passion to your life. It provides lasting value that will lift your life more often to the "upper end" of happiness.[3]

As ministers we have a calling. So we must let the changes that need to take place happen. Get ready to reach the upper ends of happiness. Wherever you are in the process, don't struggle with change as I did. Embrace it— make the most of it so that you can enjoy the rest of your life. For those who embrace it, retiring is like putting on a new set of Michelins—get ready for the ride of your life. Since change is going to happen, prepare for it. Then when it comes, enjoy it.

In closing this chapter I want once again to refer to Wes Tracy's excellent statements in his book *Younger than I Used to Be*. I'm taking the liberty to paraphrase a segment from page 20: "Some retired ministers have to work; others want to work. Either way, it will not be the same as it was when you were pastoring a church. Try a new ministry. Find a need and fill it rather than letting life slowly empty you of meaning." Tracy then quotes Stephen Covey: "If you want to die early, retire to golf and fishing, and sit around swallowing prescriptions and occasionally seeing your grandkids."[4]

Make up your mind now to plan some adjustments in your life. Since change is inevitable, make it your friend.

2
MINISTRY NEVER ENDS

One of the good things about being called into ministry is that it's a lifetime call. As I've already stated, retirees are no longer able to carry the heavy load of pastoring. However, that fact does not automatically mandate an end to ministry. There are a multitude of areas in which we can continue to serve.

We may need to be infected with the attitude of Billy Graham, who, when approached about retirement, is reported to have responded that he never read anywhere in the Bible that a prophet of the Lord retired. So he continued holding crusades until his health mandated stopping at the age of 84.

You can be sure that although he is no longer physically able to stand in the pulpit and preach for crusades, Dr. Graham will continue to be involved in some way in ministry. You see, he loves serving God in any way that he can. As a matter of fact, he spoke in March 2006 for a two-day Celebration of Hope event in New Orleans. Although he is physically weak, there is still a fire burning in his heart that ignites him to continue with the call God laid on his heart many years ago.

What Is Christian Retirement?

On the Web site www.gotquestions.org, powerful attention is drawn to the question "What is the Christian view of retirement?"

Even though one may retire from one's work (even "full-time" Christian ministry), he should never retire from serving the Lord. (The *way* that they serve Him may change.) You have the example of two very old people in Luke 2:25-38 (Simeon and Anna) who continued to serve the Lord faithfully. In that passage you have an elderly widow who is spoken of as *ministering* to the Lord (it uses a word usually reserved for priestly service) in the temple daily with fastings and prayer. Indeed, Titus 2 states that the older men and women are to teach those younger than them how to behave by their example.[1]

They further state, "One's older years are *NOT* to be spent on the pursuit of pleasure. . . . Contrary to biblical instruction, most people equate retirement with 'pursuit of pleasure' if at all possible!"

The Web site makes a strong summary statement:

As one reaches "retirement age" (whatever that is), his vocation may change, but living one's life to serve the Lord does not change. And often it is these "senior saints" who, having a lifetime of walking with God, are able to relate the truths of God's Word in shoe leather by relating how God has worked in their lives. The psalmist's prayer should be our prayer as we age (Psalm 71:18): "Now also when I am old and grey-headed, O God, forsake me not; *until I have showed thy strength unto this generation and thy power to every one that is to come*" (emphasis added).[2]

A Valuable Service

Rather than being condemned to ride off into the sunset, retired pastors can make valuable contributions to the Kingdom. Five months before my graduation from seminary, I received a call from John L. Knight, who was at that time the district superintendent for the Church of the Nazarene in Florida. He informed me that I had been called to pastor the church at Sebring, Florida. I explained to him that I had five more months of school and could not come before graduation. I can still hear his response: "That's no problem, Gene. I have old Brother Melton, an

87-year-old retired pastor, who'll keep the church alive until you can get there." And that retiree did just that.

Now suppose that retired pastor had taken the attitude "I've retired. I've done my part. I don't want to carry that load anymore." The Sebring church could have died because there was no one else to lead. However, because an 87-year-old still had some fire in his heart for ministry, there's a strong, thriving church today in that beautiful little city. That old warhorse rendered a valuable service for the Kingdom. He did not build the church, but he certainly helped keep it alive.

There is no reason in the world that we retired ministers can't help keep some churches alive. In large cities with institutions of higher learning, many supply ministers are available to fill church pulpits. But in countless smaller areas it still takes some of us ants who can't do what we used to do but can still make some contribution to the Kingdom. Our load is smaller, but we can make a difference.

In some instances we can move in and meet the need by serving as interim pastors. In other situations we can drive out to cover a pulpit on Sunday. In either case, that is a vital service for the Kingdom.

Minister to Your Pastor

Another area in which we can make a difference is by pastoring the pastor of our local church. Who pastors your pastor? When retirement came my way, the Lord said, "I want you to do some of the things you wish someone had done for you when *you* were pastoring."

When I was in the full-time pastorate, many times I needed someone to pastor me—someone to simply say something positive. I had a lot of critics and complainers, but not as many who strengthened and encouraged me.

Fortunately, I grew up in church. I often recall a sign that hung to the right of the pulpit in the church I attended in Nashville. It read, "Pray for the only member of this congregation who has no pastor." Frankly, at that time the sign was confusing to me. I thought H. H. Wise, who was our pastor, was everyone's pastor. Later, after God called me into ministry, I truly understood the essence of the message of that sign. Pastors simply cannot pastor themselves.

Following Dr. Wise's death, his widow gave that sign to me and said, "Now that you understand what this means, Harry would be happy for you to have it." I still have that sign hanging in my office.

It is a rare but beautiful situation when there is someone to pastor the pastor—someone who prays, supports, compliments, and encourages him or her. Usually, when that happens it comes from a very special layperson. Why not from a clergyperson who has been where the pastor is?

As a result of my experiences and realization of the need, Shepherds' Fold Ministries was founded. Our sole purpose is to encourage and affirm pastors, spouses, and their families. It's wonderful to realize when we have helped encourage pastors. We love to see the light go on in their eyes when they realize someone who understands the load they carry thinks they're doing a good job.

You don't have to start a new organization in order to

pastor your pastor. Just start praying and openly expressing your love for him or her. Use your influence to help the congregation understand the load that is carried by God's shepherd for that flock. Each one of us is an attitude-carrier. Start a campaign to infect the congregation with a positive attitude of support for your pastor.

Many people have no idea what is involved in leading a church. In one of my churches there was a gentleman who regularly came by the parsonage to help me pass the time between Sundays. He thought I had a lot of time on my hands.

You would be surprised to know the people where you attend are also that naive about pastoral responsibilities and time constraints. It is a great service to render to your pastor, the Kingdom, and people who don't understand when you help them open their eyes to the situation.

In his book *Finish Strong*, Richard Capen Jr. quotes theologian William Barclay: "One of the highest of human duties is the duty of encouragement. . . . It is easy to laugh at men's ideals; it is easy to pour cold water on their enthusiasm; it is easy to discourage others. The world is full of discouragers. Many a time a word of praise or thanks or appreciation or cheer has kept a man on his feet. Blessed is the man who speaks such a word."[3]

And we can be the person to speak those encouraging words.

Don't Be a Burden

I don't know that I call what Aaron and Hur did for Moses in Exod. 17 to be "pastoring their pastor," but it sure made a difference in the situation at hand. Remember that story?

The Amalekites came and attacked the Israelites at Rephidim. Moses said to Joshua, "Choose some of our men and go out to fight the Amalekites. Tomorrow I will stand on top of the hill with the staff of God in my hands." So Joshua fought the Amalekites as Moses had ordered, and Moses, Aaron and Hur went to the top of the hill. As long as Moses held up his hands, the Israelites were winning, but whenever he lowered his hands, the Amalekites were winning. When Moses' hands grew tired, they took a stone and put it under him and he sat upon it. Aaron and Hur held his hands up— one on one side, one on the other—so that his hands remained steady until sunset. So Joshua overcame the Amalekite army with the sword (vv. 8-13).

Moses was God's man for that particular crisis. Aaron and Hur were the ants who made him effective. The battle was won because they did what they could. They supported God's man.

Your pastor may very well be walking in Moses' sandals. There's no doubt there is a battle going on for the eternal souls of the people God loves where you attend church. What a wonderful blessing it will be when you go to your Moses and say, "Let me help you." You can at least be one of those who help to hold up your pastor's hands while he or she does the work God has assigned for that congregation.

Unfortunately, some retirees feel it is their calling to keep their pastor in line and humble. Second-guessing and criticism may feed their ego, but it will not build the Kingdom.

I have just visited a church where God is blessing His people and exciting things are happening. A vibrant pastor is leading his congregation in a major relocation project. They must move from their inner-city, landlocked location to continue to grow.

God has miraculously given this church a prime piece of property in a growing part of town. Also, He has given them the finances to build on their new property. So why is a retired pastor in that congregation calling church members to criticize the project, saying, "This preacher will kill our church"? The retiree had never pastored a church half the size of that one. He never led a building project that would compare to it. Could it be that he is jealous of the success of that young pastor? I don't know the answer, but I do know he has taken a perilous route if he cares anything about advancing the Kingdom.

There may be times when we need to speak up and raise questions. However, it must always be done prayerfully, discreetly, and in a spirit of love after getting clearance from God.

Still Think It's Over?

If you're one of those retirees who thinks ministry is over, you need to do some serious rethinking. Ministry is over only when we want it to end. Age is not the determining factor—attitude is.

I like the attitude reflected by George Bernard Shaw:

I want to be thoroughly used up when I die,
For the harder I work, the more I live.

Life is a sort of splendid torch which I hold for a moment.
And I want to make it burn brightly,
Before I hand it off to future generations.

It's no wonder Richard Capen Jr. gave those words a prominent place in his book *Finish Strong*.[4]

Capen goes on to write about one who demonstrated Shaw's attitude. "Woody Wirt, former editor of DECISION magazine, published his twenty-sixth book at age 85. Most have been about joy; all have been about staying young. One of his titles is a classic: *I Don't Know What Old Is, But Old Is Older Than Me*. In two sentences, he has captured the essence of agelessness: 'The number one problem with us older people is a lack of vision. We are immortal until the vision fades.'"[5]

Apparently, Norman Vincent Peale was another one of those ministers who loved the calling God had given him. He seemed never to tire of his service for God. Dave Thomas, founder of Wendy's hamburger chain, served on the board of *Guideposts* magazine with Dr. Peale. In his book *Well Done!* Thomas paid a ringing tribute to a minister who loved his calling:

Dr. Norman loved to give talks. It seemed that no audience ever gave Norman Vincent Peale the jitters. He thrived on being able to lift big crowds up, to give them the right attitude. While most of us—almost all of us—need a friendly, warmed-up audience to give a good talk, Dr. Norman had the gift of taking any audience and making it his audience.

When he was ninety-four he made his last big speech at the yearly commencement of Ohio Wesleyan University. He talked for twenty-five minutes without a single note in front of 2,000 people. It was a red-letter day for Norman—72 years almost to the hour after receiving his own diploma from the same college.

Mrs. Ruth [Peale] said he grew weaker after that event. Over the days and months that followed, he stayed at home mostly, and the strength kind of went out of him day by day—the strength but not the spirit. Not the fun either. One morning their daughter, Margaret, was helping to feed Dr. Norman. His eyes lit up— as only Norman's could—and he said in a clear voice, *No more oatmeal!*[6]

Need one more example of older people whose fire may burn low but still have some heat? On Anthony Bradley's Web site, he states, "See—some Christians don't really retire." He then illustrates the point with the following story.

Ray Crist, a retired scientist who started teaching at Messiah College near Harrisburg in 1970, put down his pointer Tuesday at age 104. At the age of 102 he became the oldest employee in the country, the AP reports. Next, Crist plans to keep up with his research and academic papers on plants and toxicity.[7]

So for many who love what they are doing, I will borrow a phrase heard often in the world of sports, "It ain't over till it's over."

Small Becomes Great

One reason many retiring ministers just quit is because they think that since they can no longer serve in a major way, then what they can do is not important. As you watch a colony of ants work, you'll notice that each individual ant is very small, and the load each carries is minuscule. A critic looking on at one or two of those tiny workers might say, "They're not accomplishing much." However, when each ant does his or her part, a significant difference occurs.

I was standing near a colony of fire ants one day. Believe me—they made a major impression on me. At first I didn't notice them, but then they decided I should move. Once they started biting me, I complied. One bite wasn't too bad. But when the whole colony went to work on me, I moved quickly. I was much bigger, but they attacked me like an army of millions. I was not about to stay in their territory.

Consider this. I weigh over 200 pounds. The ants were so tiny their weight could not be measured. In fact, the entire colony all put together amounted to only a tiny fraction of my weight. However, when they each did what they could, this big old, heavy body of mine was no match for them. Small became great in its effect upon me.

Again I emphasize that we retirees may be individually small and unable to carry much of a load. However, when we each do what we're capable of doing, we demonstrate the truth of that great old song "Little Is Much When God Is in It," by Kittie L. Suffield:

In the harvest field now ripened
  There's a work for all to do;
Hark! the voice of God is calling
  To the harvest calling you.

Does the place you're called to labor
  Seem so small and little known?
It is great if God is in it,
  And He'll not forget His own.

Are you laid aside from service,
  Body worn from toil and care?
You can still be in the battle
  In the sacred place of prayer.

When the conflict here is ended
  And our race on earth is run,
He will say, if we are faithful,
  "Welcome home, My child—well done!"

Little is much when God is in it!
  Labor not for wealth or fame.
There's a crown—and you can win it,
  If you go in Jesus' name.

So let your ministry go on. You may be well past the golden age of 65 years, but ministry should not—indeed, *must* not—end. There *is* something you can do for the Kingdom.

3
BARRIERS TO
BE OVERCOME

While ministry goes on, there are some serious adjustments to be made. Except in a very few situations, there are some major hurdles in the way of a pleasant retirement. I believe the most critical is the emotional battle of discovering a new identity. While we need not disconnect from our past, neither can we depend on our past for our present value.

Be sure you are ready for retirement before taking that step. If, like me, you didn't choose retirement and retirement chose you, you may need to reconsider how you're going to live out this experience.

In a very insightful book, *When Christians Retire*, Dwight Hervey Small, a Christian sociologist, writes, "Retirement can be either a dream or a disaster."[1] Unfortunately, for many ministers retirement is a disaster. Failure to make proper preparations catches up with them, and inability to adjust frustrates them. In some situations, finances are a major problem. For others, it is the issue of identity. For some retirees, it is the matter of health. And still other retirees struggle to make the best use of their newly found free time.

Dr. Small goes on to ask a series of searching questions:

Exactly what is so promising about retirement? There's no contract that spells out the details, no blueprint that seems to fit everyone. So how do we know what to expect? What if gains do not outweigh losses? What about psychological costs down the road? What about major social adjustments? Can we handle it all without some mental turmoil? What are your own hopes and dreams? And more importantly, around what center will your life be organized? Is there productive life after a career ends? If so, of what kind? How should you restructure your new world?[2]

The answers to some of these questions may help prevent many retirees' dreams from turning into nightmares. However, if we can get over some of the obstacles that can come between ourselves and a happy retirement, our best dreams may yet come true.

Barrier No. 1: Who Am I?

Regardless of the size of the church you pastored or the ministry you led, you were the CEO. Most of us who were pastors don't really think of ourselves in that manner, but that is the position we filled. This fact also means we were in a very special role. People looked up to us, valued our advice, and we derived a certain amount of our self-worth from that identity.

So when you retire and lose that identity, what happens? How much golf can you play, and how many fish can you catch before it gets old and boring? Believe me, I love to do both but I get weary of them. I also love gardening, but after a while that, too, gets tiresome.

Frankly, I find my satisfaction and pleasure in a variety of things, but none is as rewarding as doing something for the Kingdom. I love to help struggling pastors and small churches, and they seem to appreciate the help. I'm one of those who think two weeks is about the ideal length of retirement. After that it gets boring.

So can life be meaningful in retirement? Can it have significant value? Absolutely! Take it from someone who had to climb over the obstacle of personal identity.

Joyce and I chose to stay in the city in which I had pastored for more than 26 years. Because of that choice, it was not unusual to run into people I had pastored or who knew me as Pastor Williams. We were determined not to be a problem to my successor, so we did none of the pastoral things—weddings, funerals, and so on. And we deliberately attended other churches.

Still, when we met people who recognized us, we were usually greeted with "Hello, Pastor. How are both of you doing?" Initially, I struggled about my response to that question. I was no longer a pastor. The "Rev." or "Dr." titles were too stilted for me. So what should I be called?

I have had a lot of fun with my solution. Finally I started jokingly telling them, "Just call me 'Father.'" After all, I still have my kids. What started out as an identity crisis has now lost its pressure. In fact, they can call me anything. For me identity is no longer a problem.

Whoever you determine you are, whatever you decide to be called, remember these words from Dwight Small:

> I am persuaded there is indeed "life after retirement" for those who seek His leading and empowering. There are opportunities for "creative usefulness," even when your circle of influence is limited. He wants us to be His partners just where we are.[3]

I don't know about you, but I am content to be His child, His partner, His messenger. Even though I had been involved in the preaching ministry for over 50 years and had spent countless hours as a pastor, that is not who I *am*. Although it may be who I *was*, life has changed. My assignment has changed. God still has plans for me as He said in Jer. 29:11: "'I know the plans I have for you,' declares the LORD, 'plans to prosper you and not to harm you, plans to give you hope and a future.'"

Frankly, I love who I am now just as much as I did when I was Pastor Williams. And once we make the adjustment from who we were to who we are, we can clear this first major hurdle with flying colors.

Barrier No. 2: What Do I Do?

You've probably heard retired people say this many times, and if you're like I was before I retired, you find it hard to believe as well: "I'm busier now than I was before I retired." A retired friend of mine once told me, "I need to get a job again so I can slow down and get some rest."

Sure, there are some people who retire with enough finances and good health that they can spend all their time on the road, at the golf course, or at the lake. A few find good, comfortable rocking chairs and snooze their lives away.

How boring! I can't imagine a more unrewarding way to spend my retirement years. Don't misunderstand me. I love golfing, fishing, traveling, gardening, and all that goes with recreational activities. However, nothing is as rewarding as being involved in ministering to God's people. God called me to be a minister, and He did not cancel His call on my life when I retired. And frankly, I just love what I'm doing.

Now and then my kids or one of my friends will ask me, "With the schedule you and Joyce keep, what's the advantage of being retired?" I believe my answer to that question speaks to the heart of the whole retirement issue. I simply explain to them that when I'm tired, don't feel good, or simply don't want to do what's requested of me, I can say no, and no one can fire me. I'm finally the captain of the ship of my life. I make my own schedule.

However, I love staying busy, and that gives my life purpose and satisfaction.

I'm in total agreement with Wes Tracy, who wrote, "A good dose of 'helper's high' may be better than all the antidepressants your doctor can scribble out on his or her prescription pad."[4]

The key phrase is "helper's high." Remember—we're an army of ants, and ants are helpers. They don't carry the entire load. And in most cases they shoulder a very small package. But each ant helps the others.

The reason so many retirees spend these wonderful years in depression is due to the fact that they are not helping anyone. Tracy goes on to state, "Study after study shows that people who volunteer live longer and stay happier."[5] He then quotes from a major study. While that study was not directed toward retired ministers, the principles the study revealed are certainly applicable.

George E. Vaillant concludes his massive Harvard study that traced 824 men for eighty years by quoting Edmund Sandford's observation written more than one hundred years ago: "The real secret of a happy old age [is] . . . service for others carried on to the end of life—a service which . . . gives perennial interest to life by making the old man [or woman] a participant in the lives of those around him and . . . surrounds him with love in return."[6]

So any way we look at it, retired people who get involved have better health, live better lives, and are all around more content than those who do not.

It would seem that ministers would not need to be prodded to continue some degree of service; however, this is not always the case. Many look forward to the day when they can get out from under the pressures of ministry. The facts are, they never fully enjoyed pastoring, so retirement comes as a relief. And you will not be surprised to know that in many cases they discover very little pure joy in their retirement years.

On the other hand, many retirees have found richly rewarding ways to stay in ministry. For them, life is still exciting. While working on this chapter, I received a letter from one of the most excited retirees you could ever meet.

Norma Jean Meredith lives in a mobile home in a rural Kansas town with a population of about 1,500. She and her husband, Dwight, traveled over 50 years in the field of evangelistic ministry, covering over 2 million miles in a variety of automobiles and visiting all 48 continental states. Dwight passed away 8 years ago. You would think Norma Jean would be depressed. Not a chance! What does this 81-year-old widowed minister do? I want to share a portion of her letter with you:

Dear ones,

Good to see you again. I enjoyed the picts and message about India. I'm sure ya'll were a blessing.

I am doing "okay" for an "old" woman nearing eighty-one. Mercy! God has been/is good to me—have no real complaint. Don't feel that old.

Had a call from Attica, Kansas, Care Home to do a Bible study every two weeks starting March 14, along with the one at Anthony, Kansas, each Saturday soon after winter months are over. Fill in at the piano every fourth Sunday. I am hoping to get "organized" for a large yard sale when it warms up some more.

I pray daily for you, that all needs will be supplied and that you'll have protection in all ways.

My love, thoughts, and prayers.

Norma Jean

Note: there is not one hint of despair or even boredom. The day I called Norma Jean to get permission to print her letter, she sounded more alive and excited than some 40-year-old friends of mine. She must have been on a "helper's high"! Having a purpose in life and a reason to stay alive does that for us.

On November 5, 2005, the Kansas City Star published a full-page story about retired ministers who have leaped over the hurdle of "What do I do?" The article is titled "Ministry for Life." Bill Tammeus interviewed an 83-year-old retired Presbyterian minister named Myron Wheeler who along with another group of retired clergymen has found meaningful things to do. He writes:

Myron volunteers three mornings a week helping to build houses for needy people and one day a week at a hospital information desk. James P. Keleher teaches part-time at a seminary.

Russell E. Money teaches Sunday school and volunteers at a medical center in a program designed to improve long-term care for the elderly.

They are among thousands of clergy in this country who fill their retirement years with more ministry.[7]

The reporter continues to describe Myron Wheeler. "As a volunteer at Habitat for Humanity of Kansas City, he [Wheeler] says, 'I've mixed concrete, I've dug ditches, I've put up walls, I've done drywall, painting, cleaning kitchen cabinets, plumbing.'"[8]

The article concludes with this insight into hurdling the obstacle of "What do I do?" He writes:

As Myron Wheeler thinks about his retirement years, he says he is grateful for the chance to help out with good causes behind the scenes.

"I'm so glad to do something that is a supporting thing," he says. "The joy of life is in enabling and supporting. I am a poor spectator. I don't enjoy sitting and watching. I just love to be active."[9]

Did you catch what Myron said? "The joy of life is in enabling and supporting." If we really want to enjoy the rest of our lives, we need to find a need and fill it.

Ministry should be, indeed must be, for life. If our physical health allows us, we must find some service and/or ministry we can perform for the benefit of someone else. Most churches need Sunday School teachers. We are trained to teach, so we should make ourselves available. Many churches need help with visitation and pastoral care. That's right down our alley. We know how to make people feel welcome when they come into the church. So we can help with greeting them.

Whatever we do, we must build a bridge to our pastor. Let him or her know that we are a friend and supporter rather than a critic. Pray with and for your pastor regularly.

It is true that some pastors, because of their own insecurity or bad experiences with some other retired ministers, may hold us at arm's length. However, love, prayer, and positive support on our part will not only open opportunities but also make us a blessing to our church. Plus, "He who is a blessing is always blessed himself."

Barrier No. 3: Where Do I Live?

On the surface we would not think this should be a critical issue. But where we choose to live after retirement can be a major decision. The difficulty is really exacerbated if, as is true in many situations, we do not own our own home. The fact is, for many of us who entered ministry in the good old days, this could be a very critical issue.

At the time I went into full-time ministry, our church not only owned the parsonage but also owned all of the furniture in that parsonage. My wife and I were 40 years old before we owned anything. As mentioned earlier, when I turned 50, it dawned on me that when I turned 65 we could be out on the street. So I requested a housing allowance, and our church graciously provided that for us. Finally we would at least have some equity with which to work when retirement time arrived. If it had not been for the church's generosity in allowing us to take that step, our retirement years would certainly be much less pleasant than they are.

Hopefully, churches are doing better on this issue. Still, when retirement time comes, whether you choose to live in your own home, to rent, or to purchase your own home for the first time, the initial question to be answered is "Where shall I live?"

Multitudes of retirees have opted for warmer climates like those of Arizona, California, Texas, and Florida. In fact, some reports indicate that while over 50 percent will move into a new home, 44 percent of them want to locate in a southern area. Many others have retired in the vicinity of a college or university.

Where you locate may be determined by your financial condition. Property in the more exotic locations in Arizona and Florida is considerably more expensive than it would be in numerous other areas. Before making a final decision about where to live, you might want to consider the results (ranked by importance) of a subscriber survey reported in 2003 in the magazine *Where to Retire* that asked, "What are your requirements for the 'good life'? What is non-negotiable if you are choosing a place to live?"

1. Low crime rate
2. Active, clean, safe downtown
3. Good hospitals nearby
4. Low overall tax rate
5. Mild climate
6. Friendly, like-minded neighbors
7. Scenic beauty nearby
8. Low cost of living
9. Good recreational facilities
10. Low housing cost
11. Active social/cultural environment
12. Nearby airport with commercial service
13. Major city nearby
14. No state income tax

15. Continuing-care retirement communities available
16. Friends, relatives in area
17. Full- or part-time employment opportunities
18. College town with adult education available[10]

To this list I would add church and worship opportunities and healthy family relationships. For me it was extremely important that I be located near my family, with whom I have a very healthy relationship. Most of our children, grandchildren, and great-grandchildren live within a three-hour drive or less from our home. Some are much farther away, but we still have the opportunity to be with them often.

More important than the convenient location is the loving relationship we enjoy. While that relationship is the result of years of nurturing, it is also there because Joyce and I do not attempt to dominate their time. They have their lives—we have ours. This relationship is enjoying proximity.

When approaching the hurdle of where to locate, I believe these six things should be carefully considered:

1. Where is the most economically feasible place for me to live?
2. Can I afford to live the lifestyle I desire there?
3. Will this location provide convenient healthcare when I need it?
4. How will this location affect my family relationship?
5. Will it permit continued spiritual growth?
6. Will there be opportunities for service to the Kingdom?

Where we decide to locate may not be exactly where we have dreamed of living. But it may prevent future nightmares. Present enjoyment is more vital than fulfilling past dreams. If you get over this hurdle successfully, you'll find you're well on your way to a meaningful retirement.

Barrier No. 4: How Do I Maintain Financial Stability?

For many retirees, maintaining financial stability may be the highest hurdle of all. In fact, I thought of addressing finances at the beginning of this chapter, but while many face this obstacle, not everyone does. Some ministerial retirees have been blessed with adequate financial arrangements. However, all of us will have to determine who we are, how we will spend our time, and where we will live. So I decided to address those hurdles first.

Since retirement in some form will come to everyone if we live long enough, those who make adequate preparation are wise. I will discuss in a later chapter ways of doing that for those who are still in the retirement pipeline.

The question before us at this point is, "How do I find some reasonable degree of financial income so that I can maintain a satisfactory lifestyle?" While many retirees have dreams of never working again, those who follow that route are in the minority. Most retirees in any profession work at least part-time. So we ministers who work at something are part of the majority.

In his book *How to Retire Happy*, Stan Hinden discusses why some people continue to work after retirement. "The line between work and retirement is becoming more blurred all the time. The fact is that many people who retire go back to work part-time—some even full-time. People are living longer and want to remain involved and productive."[11]

Hinden points to two important surveys:

> Two national surveys show that we can expect an explosion of part-time retired workers in the years ahead. That's because members of the baby-boom generation—77 million people born between 1946 and 1964—will begin to retire in 2010.[12]

According to these surveys, "relatively small numbers of people said they expected to work because they needed the money." Rather, most wanted to pursue personal goals. Many even planned to "start their own businesses."[13]

When you read the lines "relatively small numbers of people said they expected to work because they needed the money," you will want to remember that those surveys were conducted among laypersons. You will notice in my survey of retired ministers, most of them work because they need the income to maintain a reasonable standard of living.

I hope you did not opt out of Social Security when you had the opportunity. Across the years, some financial planners encouraged ministers to exercise that option and leave the program to set up their own retirement funds. Now some of those retirees are really hurting, especially for medical coverage. Social Security has received much negative press, but I'm convinced it will always be there for those who have contributed to it. Frankly, I am very grateful that Medicare and Medicaid are in my retirement portfolio.

Health and opportunity permitting, there's no reason not to work at least part-time. Hinden quotes Neal Cutler, former director of Survey Research at the National Council on Aging in Washington, D.C.:

We will see more and more people who describe themselves as retired, but continue to work. . . . Many of these people are working by choice, not because they have to. In the twenty-first century, retirement will encompass a wide range of options. We will see some 75-year-olds working two jobs and some 40-year-olds lounging poolside.

Retirement . . . used to be defined by what one was no longer doing—not parenting, not working, not actively involved. Increasingly it will be defined by what one does do—second career, volunteer work, travel, sports activity. [14]

One of the major problems faced by respondents to my survey of retired ministers was the lack of financial support. Overcoming this may take energy and ingenuity, but you can do it. Many retired ministers have gotten involved in secular work where they discovered a plethora of opportunities to be used of God. Some are chaplains in extended care homes. Others take part-time jobs that involve them with young people. You are willing to be used of God, aren't you? Then take advantage of any opportunity He gives you. There is nothing in the world like realizing that God has used you for His glory. If that is in some sort of secular work, so be it!

You may need help to actually put food on the table, but our Heavenly Father always has His spiritual table loaded and ready for you to enjoy. So come to the table and enjoy the feast He has prepared for you.

Barrier No. 5: How Do I Handle Health Issues?

Health issues for the retiree and/or spouse can be critical. In many situations health problems have already become serious before retirement. And leaving full-time employment only exacerbates the issue. Health can contribute to or be a major hindrance in retirement years. Some retirees become full-time caregivers for a spouse who is in ill health. And this hurdle will have a powerful influence on all plans and activities for what should be the golden years.

I have a very dear friend who recently retired and is dealing with this situation. After many years as a successful pastor and educator, age and health caught up with him. While his mind remained as sharp as ever, his body simply began to break down. In addition, his loving spouse had a serious illness that required his total attention and care.

When I first heard of his impending retirement, I thought, "Great! Now he can be free to be a blessing to many people in a lot of places. There are revivals and all kinds of ministries in which he can participate." It didn't happen like that. Between his failing health and his wife's already failed health, traveling to minister to others is all but impossible. In fact, he gives most of his time as a constant caregiver to his mate.

That could cause a person to be bitter—maybe even question God's kindness. Not so with my friend! He believes the ministry God has given to him at this point in his life is to care for his loving companion, who faithfully spent her younger, healthier years faithfully by his side serving the

Lord and the Church. Rather than becoming bitter, as my survey indicated some retirees with problems do, he has determined to be faithful and find some pleasure in what is an extremely difficult and challenging situation. Maybe he heard someone say, "Happiness is a choice" and chose to find joy rather than despair.

In addressing the health issue in his book *Get a Life*, Ralph Warner writes:

> I find it odd that although most people currently in midlife say that after retirement they hope to count themselves among the active, energized group, a great many follow a lifestyle that almost guarantees they will be in such poor physical condition they will spend most of their retirement on a couch. Even odder is the fact that many sedentary middle-aged people whose health and stamina are already in obvious decline nevertheless quickly and cheerfully agree that staying physically active is a key factor to enjoying retirement. . . .
>
> Don't just take my word for it. John Rowe, a gerontologist and president of Mt. Sinai Medical Center, puts it like this: "Only about 30 percent of the characteristics of aging are genetically based; the rest—70 percent—are not. . . . People are largely responsible for their own old age."[15]

Please note that last sentence—"People are largely responsible for their own old age." Everyone recognizes that some situations are totally out of our control. As human beings, our bodies wear out and get sick. But most of us can do a better job of taking care of ourselves and thereby enjoy our retirement more fully. In many situations, we can do something to bridge the health barrier to a meaningful retirement.

We need to stay as active as our physical condition permits. Since we don't have to be at the office by 9 A.M., why not take a good walk every morning? Joyce and I have discovered that we can walk about two miles in 30 to 35 minutes. We have also learned that this simple exercise increases our energy level. When weather prohibits our ability to walk outdoors, we go to the mall and walk "with those old people." This simple, nonstressful exercise has paid great dividends for us.

Many of us have stiff joints and weak muscles. These things may tempt us to do nothing but sit around. However, doing that only makes us stiffer and weaker—adding to our problems. Why not join a water aerobics class, where you can exercise your body and also interact with others who share similar physical challenges?

A good number of responders to my survey of ministerial retirees remain active by gardening or woodworking. The important thing is to keep our bodies moving as much as possible. Every health and aging study I have seen points out that it's critical to stay as physically active as our bodies will permit.

Also, one more helpful resource to maintaining good health is to learn and maintain a healthful, well-balanced diet. Again, I turn to Ralph Warner in *Get a Life*. In a section titled "Clean Up Your Diet" he writes:

> Most of us already understand that we should be eating far healthier meals. Take a look at your dinner plate;

it should contain no more than a few ounces of lean meat, but plenty of vegetables. . . . Eating lots of fruits, vegetables, and whole grains, and cutting way back on fatty, salty, and sugary foods, is an obvious way to do better. And for men, a number of studies show that consuming lycopene-rich foods such as pink grapefruit and cooked tomatoes is a sensible strategy to reduce the likelihood of developing prostate cancer.[16]

So, there it is—help yourself to better health and a better life.

I fully recognize the problems of health and aging and the barrier these issues can raise to meaningful retirement years. However, remember—in only 30 percent of these situations are the problems genetically based. In the other situations years of failure to take health care seriously have finally caught up with them. However, attitude is a choice even in those cases in which the retiree has no control over his or her physical conditions.

My mother is 100 years old. She still lives alone. Her body has put her through all kinds of physical challenges— broken hips, double pneumonia, falls, failing eyesight and hearing, and so on. However, she still stays active in the retirement home where she lives in Madison, Tennessee. She leaves her apartment to walk and to interact with the other residents. As a result, her mind is still sharp, and she still finds many pleasures in life. She has cleared the barrier of poor health and aging. Consequently, she continues to enjoy her life of retirement.

You may not live to be 100, but you, too, can clear this

hurdle and make the most of the situation in which God has placed you. As you will see in the survey responses, health is a major factor for many retired people. But realizing that it comes to all of us who live long enough, many of the respondents have learned to maximize their remaining health rather than allow what they do not have to rob them of meaningful retirement years.

There may very well be some other obstacles in the way of a pleasant, meaningful, and fruitful retirement. I lay no claim to being an expert in this area of life. I do know that these five hurdles were the most prominent ones in the responses to my survey.

There's a good chance that if you clear the hurdles of *Who am I? What do I do? Where do I live? How do I maintain financial stability?* and *How do I handle health issues?* you'll have an excellent opportunity to enjoy your golden years. Clear all five hurdles, and I can guarantee you a wonderful remainder of your life.

4
BRIDGES TO A MEANINGFUL RETIREMENT

Since we have looked at the major barriers to a meaningful retirement, it seems only right to turn our thoughts to the positive aspects that will help us enjoy that status. I have chosen the term *meaningful retirement* very deliberately and carefully.

I believe a meaningful, fulfilling retirement is more than just passing time until we pass on. It's not a 180-degree turn from what has been the driving force in our lives. Rather, it's a life in which serious physical adjustments are made that we may practice what has been rewarding in preretirement years. There is no reason to totally black out or try to erase those preretirement experiences. Rather, we learn to adjust and pass on to others, as health and opportunities permit, the lessons we have learned along with the joys we have experienced.

While I was working on this chapter, I saw a commercial featuring Reggie Jackson. For many years Reggie was known as "Mr. October" because of his heroics on the baseball field. He has five world championship rings that are his primarily because of his ability to hit a baseball. He has long since quit playing. Age and physical conditions mandated his retirement. However, there Reggie was in that commercial talking to young men about the basics of hitting a ball. I understand he was probably paid quite handsomely for the ad. Yet he still had so much excitement in his voice that I wanted to go out and purchase the hitting machine he was recommending.

It was Reggie's attitude that made me want what he was sponsoring. And I promise you that many parents are in debt because their kids want to be like Reggie Jackson who not only experienced an exciting past but is also enjoying a very meaningful present.

The Key

The key to finding and crossing the bridges to a meaningful present is *attitude*. In reading over 300 responses to my survey on ministerial retirement I could not escape the clear difference in attitude that was reflected throughout those responses. It was ironic one day to open some surveys and read, "I'm having the time of my life. I have no complaints. The church has been good to my wife, four sons, and me. I appreciate the basic pension and the chance to invest in the annuity program." In that same bundle of responses I read, "After all the years I spent in the ministry raising budgets, etc., I feel like the district and general church leaders have forgotten me. They never contact me. I feel put on the shelf and forgotten." These two attitudes reflect totally opposite positions.

I fully understand that some retirees have very different, more difficult circumstances than others. For many, the financial pressure and loss of identity are emotionally destructive. Still, the evidence is clear—we have a choice in how we respond to everything that happens in our lives.

When retirement time came for me, I would have been very happy with a pension in line with some secular retirement plans I've heard about that are equal to 50 to 65 percent of salary earned during active years of service. As a pastor, my package wasn't even close. Still, I'm so very grateful for what I receive each month. When my father retired from the factory where he had worked for 35 years, he received no retirement funds at all. He was given a watch and Social Security. So I choose to make the most of what I have that I may be able to cross that bridge to a meaningful life.

Sometimes we wonder why some people have a more positive attitude than others. According to Ralph Warner, whether people are in retirement or not, "some people just seem to get more enjoyment out of life than others."[1]

So perhaps the reason some retirees struggle with their attitudes is because they were struggling before they reached that milestone. It's clear in almost every work on retirement that a positive attitude will make a significant difference in the level of pleasure experienced. In my earlier book *In the Shadow of the Steeple: The Vital Role of the Smaller Church in a Megachurch World,* I spoke to active pastors about the effect of their attitudes on their work. I quoted one of the great pastors of our day, Chuck Swindoll. He speaks beautifully to the importance of our attitudes:

> *I believe the single most significant decision I can make on a day-to-day basis is my choice of attitude.* It is more important than my past, my education, my bankroll, my successes or failures, fame or pain, what other people think of me or say about me, my circumstances, or my position. Attitude . . . keeps me going or cripples my progress.[2]

This is good advice for retirees as well as active ministers. It is essential that we continue to look for positive things in our lives. There is power in positive thinking. And that power can help us make more out of each day than we could ever experience without it.

When my daughter, Laurel, was diagnosed with breast

cancer, I did not know how she would handle the grim news. She already had multiple sclerosis as well as an unspecified autoimmune disease. The cancer would have been strike three for many people. Laurel chose not to let that happen. When I asked her how she handled the diagnosis, she responded, "Dad, I look for and find something good every day. Even when I feel horrible, the sun comes up, our little boy, Chance, brings me a dandelion bouquet or something else good happens. It's there. I just have to look for it."

There is something good in every retiree's life. We just have to look for it. And when we find it, we will have found the way to cross the bridge to a meaningful retirement.

Any one of us, whether we are retirees or are still in full-time ministry, will find the attitude of Ron Mehl to be of great benefit. On what he thought was a routine visit to his doctor's office, he learned he had leukemia—a slow-moving form of cancer. He lived for 10 years under that penalty of death. And I mean *he lived*. He could have questioned God, become depressed, or just plain given up. Not Ron! He chose to make those years meaningful ones in ministering to his congregation. How did he do that? By taking the attitude he presents in his book *Surprise Endings*, "God delights in taking the bad things in our lives and making them into good things. For His children, everything indeed turns out right. We all live happily ever after."[3]

Evidently, Ron believed Paul was speaking the truth when he wrote in Rom. 8:28, "We know that in all things God works for the good of those who love him, who have been called according to his purpose."

I believe it. So can you. Now let us reflect that faith in the attitudes we permit to control our lives and cross the bridges that enable us to make the most of our retirement years.

Bridge No. 1: Cultivate Your Self-Respect

Self-respect is one of the most valuable assets any of us can have. The bottom line is that no one is more healthy than his or her sense of self-worth. Conversely, poor self-esteem can put us below the poverty line. Granted, some people are not as valuable as they may think they are, and their self-inflated egos make them difficult to be around. Still, many retired ministers need to get their heads up and shoulders back so they can realize how valuable they are. And that is something only each individual can do.

A typical survey response reads, "When God called us to ministry He did not have an expiration date in mind. Even in retirement there are many areas of ministry remaining."

Perhaps it will help us to realize that there are multiple areas of ministry other than pastoring. Granted, teaching a children's class is not as glamorous as being in the pulpit; however, teaching youngsters has eternal rewards.

While growing up in Nashville, I was far from being the calmest, best-behaved child in my Sunday School class. In fact, I was quite the opposite. Margaret Griggs gave of her time and energy in order to teach my kindergarten class. She sowed many seeds, and some of them bore fruit. I know there must have been times when she wondered if that class was worth her time and energy. However, she was faithful, and I'll never forget what happened once after I became a pastor and I was visiting my childhood church. Mrs. Griggs and I met face-to-face in the hallway. She grabbed me, hugged me, and said, "Gene, I'm so proud of you! I never thought you'd amount to anything!"

I'm still not sure I've amounted to anything. But Mrs. Griggs was rewarded and was rightfully proud of her contribution to my ministry. And in turn, she had an investment in every individual I've helped in over 50 years of ministry.

Experiences like teaching, helping with visitation, leading a small group, being a church greeter, and helping in multiple other assignments will help bolster our self-esteem. Participating in these ministries makes us contributors, not just takers. I like the idea of the survey responder who said, "Retirement is not a period."

In his book *When Christians Retire* Dwight Small speaks to what he calls "the status that defines us":

Stepping into retirement is stepping into an entirely different universe with a lifestyle all its own. Your personal, psychological equilibrium becomes upset, and certain familiar supports are swept away. Hopefully, a spouse or close friend becomes a support system. Different situations call for different support persons, so trust God for His choice. . . .

Harder to swallow, as Jules Willing points out, "is realization that your contributions to the professional, business, or common work world—contributions once gratefully credited to you—are no longer important to anyone besides you."[4]

So whatever self-esteem we might have because of our past

will become very fragile. However, our present self-esteem can be strong if we "find a need and fill it."

There's no question that the best way to retain and even build our self-respect is to get involved somewhere, somehow, in some kind of ministry. That involvement may be in the church, but it doesn't have to be. In my city there is a large ministry to needy people called His Helping Hands. They reach scores of needy people each week with food, clothing, furniture, and even automobiles. Everyone who receives physical, tangible help also receives some spiritual advice. This ministry is carried out by a group of retirees. In fact, if it were not for them, it wouldn't even exist.

That bunch of ants is very proud of what God is using them to accomplish. Not one of them has a problem with self-esteem. They know God is using them. They're part of the many volunteers who offer their services to help others. And these services are worth a sizeable amount. According to a 1991 Gallup poll, if the total volunteer hours of Americans were "measured in dollars," they "would be worth $176 billion."[5] Just think what that amount would be today.

We're valuable! We're partners with God in His business—changing lives. And that should help each one of us to lift our heads high. So we need to help ourselves to some healthy self-esteem by getting involved in some type of ministry.

Bridge No. 2: Develop a Hobby

It's never too late to develop a hobby. Unless physical conditions totally prohibit it, we need to find something to do that's just for fun. A hobby will not only help us pass the time but will also give us a sense of accomplishment. Many hobbies provide some much-needed exercise.

In their book *The New Retirement*, Cullinane and Fitzgerald observe, "A hobby enriches your life by increasing your knowledge, sharpening your skills, and/or bringing you inner peace."[6] None of us needs to be bored to death. So we must do ourselves a favor and get a hobby.

I was fascinated by the hobbies that showed up in the survey responses. It was not surprising that we have a great number of golfers, gardeners, fishermen, and travelers. But frankly, I was surprised at the number of woodworkers, motorcycle riders, and artists. I think the following responder spoke volumes: "I did play golf. I'm now down to checkers. I don't know what I'll do when I get old. I'm only 86!" Another retiree had just purchased a new computer and added, "Old dogs *can* learn new tricks!"

We may or may not adopt any of these hobbies, but we can do ourselves and those who love us a favor by finding one that will bring enjoyment into our lives.

Bridge No. 3: Take Care of Your Health

According to many survey responses, a large percentage of retirees suffer from health problems. Some of these are just part of the aging process. Others are the result of abusing bodies through bad diet, bad habits, or other activities from younger years. However, most retirees would improve their health in a significant way by learning to eat healthfully and exercising regularly.

Art Linkletter is a familiar name to all of us who are over the age of 65. We grew up laughing at him and with him. He has reached the wonderful age of 94 and is still very much alive and engaged in helping us enjoy life. In his great book *How to Make the Rest of Your Life the Best of Your Life*, mentioned previously, he writes:

You can be more fit than you were at thirty. It's never too late to start exercising, adopt healthy habits and reap the benefits. Studies have shown that people in their 60s, 70s, and 80s who start a regular exercise program for the first time in their lives gain just as great a benefit as younger people.[7]

While I was working on this chapter, I heard about fitness guru Jack LaLanne's attitude. Frankly, I thought he had died since I hadn't seen him on television in a long time. But he's obviously fully alive at 92 years of age. How does he stay so healthy? He eats right and works out two hours every morning even though he says he hates the workouts. He is thriving on the results of his consistent activity.

We won't get the results unless we pay the price of eating healthfully and staying physically active. Every book I have read on retirement has a lot to say on this issue. So take this good advice, and cross the bridge to a meaningful retirement.

Bridge No. 4: Take Some Lessons in Aging

All of us want to make the most of this period in our lives. It can be like the fourth quarter of a football game when many games are won or lost. So if retirement is the final quarter, what we do during this time may well determine whether we come to the end of our lives as winners or losers. I know all of us want to go out on the winning side. To do so, we'll need some help.

We prepared to make the most of the first three quarters of our lives by going to school and learning from people who were qualified to give good advice to us. Stan Hinden won a Pulitzer prize for his retirement column "Retirement Journal." Being sensitive to the subject for 20 years prepared him to offer several don'ts and dos in his book *How to Retire Happy*. Here are just a few:

The don'ts

- Don't bore your friends and relatives by talking on and on about your health problems. . . .
- Don't neglect old friends. . . .
- Don't assume that age makes you wise. . . .

The dos

- Do exercise regularly. . . .
- Do eat healthfully. . . .
- Do try to . . . develop new friendships.[8]

Learning lessons like these will help you across an important bridge to a meaningful retirement. Then, like Reggie Jackson or Jack LaLanne or many retirees who responded to my survey, you, too, will discover that these are very exciting days.

When I saw the book *Finish Strong* by Richard Capen Jr., I devoured it. The author has been a successful Christian publisher (editor of the *Miami Herald*), an ambassador under the first President Bush, and a powerful influence for

God in the professional world. He gives what he calls "headlines to live by." Here are some examples:

- Above all, cherish your family, friends, and faith in God.
- Stand up for what you believe. Life is not a popularity contest.
- Earn the trust of others. Everything in life starts with it. . . .
- No matter what chapter of life you are in, no matter what your age, start strong and finish strong. Never tolerate half-baked efforts.[9]

I'm taking the liberty of adapting the last headline for those of us who are retired ministers of the gospel. "We are in what will be the final chapter of our lives. Regardless of what page (age) we are on, be strong, finish strong, and never tolerate half-baked efforts." By implementing this strategy, we are well on our way to crossing another bridge to a meaningful ministerial retirement.

Passing the Baton

I have said several times that retirement is a process. It isn't something we do, where we put a period to the first three quarters of our lives and walk away. Those who want the final quarter to be meaningful make adjustments mentally, physically, emotionally, and, in most cases, financially.

I am in the ninth year of my retirement, and I am still making changes so that I can get the most out of my life. For example, today I tweaked my mental state in a manner that I believe will enable me to enjoy this time of my life more than ever.

I am one of those guys who has always been right in the middle of things. I loved being involved up to my ears in just about everything that was going on. I should have learned something at age 65 when, while still trying to stay active by playing softball, my body said *Enough!* I made an adjustment, quit playing, and can still walk without much pain.

Not only was I physically active, but I was also mentally engaged in almost everything. If honest confession is good for the soul, my soul is going to feel much better. I loved being on boards and committees as well as sharing the lessons I had learned in ministry as opportunities arose. I felt that I had ideas to contribute, and I wanted to be involved. Then retirement came.

Guess what! When we retire, we're no longer *on* anything. There's no platform from which we can present our great ideas. Frankly, I have struggled with that. My mind is still very active. It has not retired yet, and I hope it never will. So what do I do with all of these great ideas? I have very few opportunities to express them to the younger pastors who are carrying the responsibility of the church.

Today, in the process of living the retired life, I made a mental adjustment. Or maybe I should say, "God did the adjusting." He reminded me there comes a time when we need to pass the torch of leadership to new people with fresh ideas who may be more in tune with their generation.

I was reminded that ministry is a lot like a relay, in which each carrier of the baton reaches the end of his or her race and passes it on to another runner with fresh legs. Passing the baton can win or lose a race, so track teams work hard on such critical exchanges. The only way for the team to win is for the runner of each segment of the race to pass the baton successfully to the next runner. Then, good team members get out of the way and cheer for the person who succeeds them.

In ministry, we retirees must learn to carefully and successfully pass the baton of ministry. Our fresh teammates have been called, prepared, and are hopefully in condition to run the next leg. What really matters is not that you or I carry the baton across the finish line but that we run our portion of the race well so that the team, God's kingdom, wins. We received the baton of leadership from those who ran before us. They ran well and then moved to the bleachers to cheer us on. Now it's our turn to move to the bleachers and cheer the new runners on.

So today I've mentally ceased to be a runner. I'll be a cheerleader, water boy, or whatever. I'll do what health and opportunity permit me to do. I'll support the team. I have a lot of young Timothys to pray for, encourage, and listen to when they need to talk.

No, I probably will not be invited to be a sharer of ideas on some leadership platforms, even though I believe I still have some good ideas. However, when the last leg of the race is run, I'll join my young teammates on the winners' podium and share the ecstasy of victory with them. Until then, I intend to make the most of every opportunity retirement life offers. I'll adjust where needed to be a sincere cheerleader for some wonderful young people whom God has enlisted for His team.

Wow! My soul feels lighter already. You might want to try one of my good ideas for retired ministers. There's a place for you in the bleachers with me from which we can cheer for the young ministers who are running a great race.

Questionnaire for
Retired Ministers

5
REVIEW OF RETIRED MINISTERS' SURVEY

I have included the questionnaire that was sent to over 700 randomly selected retired ministers across the United States and Canada so that you may see how you fit into the retirement process. And make no mistake—retirement is a process. With 328 returns, the percentage of responders was well above the average from such questionnaires, which indicates a high interest in this area of need.

After the big day when you have your final celebration, there will be many adjustments to be made. Retirement is not a simple, "OK—I'm through working." Most retirees find life is more meaningful when they stay flexible and continue to make adjustments as they work through the aging process.

According to the survey, 50 percent of the respondents were in ministry 40 years or more. This statistic is significant. Ministry is a lifelong calling. When a person is involved in anything that long, he or she does not simply punch a clock and walk away. Serving God and others becomes a way of life that is not easily broken—nor should it be.

This lifelong calling may also explain why 63.1 percent were either 61 years of age before taking retirement seriously or *never* made plans for retirement. That is almost two-thirds of those involved in ministry. They were so immersed in ministry they never thought of quitting. I *do not* mean to encourage or promote this poor planning for the future. However, this fact does reflect how absorbed many who are in ministry become in their calling. We will soon see that this attitude of commitment also appears in other parts of the survey, but before we do that, let's take look at the actual questionnaire to see how the respondents answered specific questions:

Questionnaire for Retired Ministers

(Percentages throughout this report may not total 100 percent due to rounding. Surveys were mailed to a random sample [713] of retired Nazarene ministers in the United States and Canada. At the time of this analysis, 328 surveys [46 percent] had been returned.)

1. **How long were you active in ministry?**

2%	Less than 10 years	5%	10 to 19 years
14%	20 to 29 years	29%	30 to 39 years
34%	40 to 49 years	16%	50 or more years

2. **How long have you been retired?**

27%	Less than 5 years	22%	5 to 9 years
22%	10 to 14 years	16%	15 to 19 years
10%	20 to 24 years	4%	25 or more years

3. **What plans did you make for retirement?**
   (Respondents were asked to indicate all appropriate answers. Therefore, the percentages total more than 100 percent.)

97%	Social Security	35%	IRA
53%	TSA/403(b)	43%	Other (Please explain.)

4. **At what age did you begin to make serious preparations for retirement?**

20%	Less than 40 years	35%	40 to 50 years
21%	50 to 60 years	12%	60+ years
12%	Never		

5. **Do you receive a denominational pension?**

96%	Yes	4%	No

6. **Are you covered by Social Security?**

99%	Yes	1%	No

7. **Are you involved in ongoing ministry?**
   (Respondents were asked to choose the most appropriate response. However, several chose more than one response. All responses were included in this analysis, so the percentages equal more than 100 percent.)

52%	Yes	26%	No
10%	Pastor	16%	Staff
3%	Parachurch	32%	Other
			(Please explain.)

8. **How do you supplement your retirement income?**

   (Some respondents did not respond to this item. The percentages reported here are of all respondents who returned a survey.)

   28% I do not need to supplement my retirement income.

   10% I am unable to supplement my retirement income.

   35% I supplement my retirement income through ministry assignments.

   3% I supplement my retirement income by writing.

   4% I supplement my retirement income by leading workshops/seminars.

   34% Other. (Please explain.)

9. **How has retirement affected your spouse?**

10. **Is health an issue in your retirement?**

    39% Yes, at this point it is a minor issue.

    27% Yes, it is a serious issue.

    30% No.

    3% Other. (Please explain.)

11. **Are you covered by health insurance?**

83%	Yes	6%	No

    11% Yes, but I worry that I will not be able to continue to afford the premiums.

12. **How important is location in your retirement?**

45%	Very important	23%	Important
20%	Fairly important	10%	Not very important
3%	Not important at all		

13. **How is your relationship with your immediate family members?**

87%	Very good	9%	Good
4%	Fairly good	0%	Not very good
0%	Not good at all		

14. **Have you found new possibilities for community involvement?**

    (Some respondents did not respond to this item. The percentages reported here are of the 296 ministers who did respond to the item.)

    54% Yes (Please describe.)   46% No

15. **How do you handle the ego challenges of no longer being a leader?**

16. **How do you maintain a warm, positive spiritual life in retirement?**

17. **Do you have hobbies you are enjoying in your retirement?**

18. **Does the pastor of the church you attend welcome you?**

85%	Yes	4%	No
12%	Somewhat		

    Does he or she use you in ministry?

46%	Yes	30%	No
25%	A little		

19. **What is the best thing for you about retirement?**

20. **What is the hardest challenge you face in retirement?**

    (Some respondents did not indicate any challenge, while others indicated more than one. The percentages reported here are of all respondents who returned a survey.)

18%	Lack of a fulfilling role	27%	Poor health
32%	Limited income	19%	Other
			(Please explain.)

21. If you were speaking to a group of young pastors, what would be your advice to help them prepare for retirement?

22. Briefly describe what retirement has meant for you.

23. Do you own your own home?
    65% Yes   18% No
    17% Yes, we have some equity in our home.

24. If you were looking for a book that would help you to get the most out of retirement, what are some of the issues that book should suggest?

25. Additional comments.

Besides the results shown, there are also important comments given in response to the survey's open-ended questions. We find again the attitude of commitment that we discussed earlier reflected in the responses to the following questions:

- Question 20: What is your hardest challenge?
- Questions 24: If you were looking for a book that would help you get the most out of retirement, what are some of the issues that book should suggest?
- Question 25: Additional comments.

Consider the responses to Question 25 these retirees (who all served 40 years or more) had to offer.

- "God is good! I'm having the time of my life."
- "At age 90 I'm having lots of fun and enjoying preaching. I preach somewhere every Sunday."
- "Be loyal and totally committed to the mission and ministry of the church."
- "Do not coast. Keep your own spiritual experience up to date."

- "Do not become cynical and sour on life."
- "Take an interest in children."
- "Stay sweet. Stay optimistic."
- "Keep a positive attitude. Always remember: God is faithful."

You will not be surprised when I tell you these positive responses came from people who are still actively involved and have hobbies.

Clearly there are lessons to be learned from these responses. If you're active in your retirement, stay involved as long as your health permits. If you're not active, find something to do and do it. People who sit around and watch the world go by have a strong tendency to be critical and cynical about what they see. They also have more health issues than those who are active.

Take a look at the survey responses. As I indicated earlier, the return was well above the normal replies to questionnaires like this one. I am grateful to those who took time to complete and return the surveys. It was impossible to report all that was written in answering the subjective questions; however, some statements stood out. I am taking the liberty of passing these replies on to you:

- Question 19: What is the best thing for you about retirement?

The overwhelming responses were freedom from the administrative demands of the church and ability to set their own schedules.

- Question 21: If you were speaking to a group of young pastors, what would be your advice to help them prepare for retirement?

Two things stood out:

(1) Start saving early, even if it's only a small amount.

(2) Buy a home or property somewhere. (In the survey, 82 percent of the responders either own their homes or have equity in one.)

- Question 22: Briefly describe what retirement has meant for you.

  No outstanding response other than some similar to those to question 9.

- Question 24: If you were looking for a book that would help you get the most out of retirement, what are some of the issues that book would suggest?

  While most of the responders had no suggestions, there were some that need to be considered. (And have had an influence on this work)

  (1) How to practice good health habits.

  (2) How to maintain self-respect in old age.

  (3) Accept the fact that you are retired and don't have to keep the same pace.

  (4) Follow the Scripture's injunction to fix your eyes on Jesus, and resist the temptation to become critical or negative.

- Question 9: How has retirement affected your spouse?

  The most consistent response was a positive one.

- Question 15: How do you handle the ego challenges of no longer being a leader?

  While some admitted to struggling initially, most

have been able to make the transition as one stated "from the pulpit to the pew."

- Question 16: How do you maintain a warm, positive spiritual life in retirement?

  Most responded that prayer and Bible study were part of their regular daily lives. I think this statement summarized all of them, "Living a consistent disciplined life of devotion."

- Question 17: Do you have hobbies you are enjoying in your retirement?

  I reported earlier that golf, gardening, fishing, and woodworking were the most popular hobbies. However, there was a large number of hunters, bike-riders, painters, and representations of almost any other hobby that could be imagined.

Take a look at the survey. Then find out where you fit in. You may be encouraged to discover where you find yourself. Remember, retirement is a process. Those who take note of this and make the needed adjustments have meaningful retirements. Those who do not make those adjustments usually suffer.

Preparing to Leave the Pulpit

6
START NOW

Now is the time to begin to make arrangements for retirement. In responding to question 21 on the retirement survey that asked, "If you were speaking to a group of young pastors, what would be your advice to help them prepare for retirement?" over 90 percent responded with some form of the advice "start early." While most of these responses referenced starting early financially, we must also recognize the need to start early in every phase of life.

A powerful work titled *Live Long and Prosper,* by Steve Vernon, includes the subtitle *Invest in Your Happiness, Health and Wealth for Retirement and Beyond.* That subtitle alerts the reader to the fact that to "live long and prosper" we need to prepare in many areas of living. In other words, retirement is a multifaceted period in our lives.

Vernon speaks strongly to our attitude toward this time in our lives:

> I think we need to replace the word *retirement* with a new concept. *Retirement* has some connotations that are no longer healthy. . . . I'd rather replace the word *retirement* with the phrase *rest-of-life.* I'm planning for *rest-of-life,* not retirement. It may be more words, but it's the same number of syllables, so it's just as easy to think and say.

> I advocate that we consciously plan for the many years that we have ahead of us. And our planning needs to go beyond finances to our health and happiness as well. We should continue to have personal growth and experiences, and not merely exist in some arrested state. Don't retreat from the world; instead, continue to remain actively engaged in life.[1]

Those who pay close attention to Vernon's advice can have a good rest-of-life by

- Planning for the years ahead
- Planning for health and happiness as well as finances
- Planning to continue personal growth experiences
- Planning to remain actively engaged in life

Whatever you might have thought of retirement in the past, remember that it's a process. While you are actively engaged in time-, energy-, and emotion-consuming ministry now, you still need to begin the process that will determine how you live the rest of your life once you step out of the pulpit.

Cullinane and Fitzgerald in their book *The New Retirement* quote Lee Iacocca, "Everybody says you've got to get ready financially. No, No! You've got to get ready psychologically."[2]

Two responses from the retirees' survey are very important to those who have not reached the rest-of-life age. In response to the question "At what age did you begin to make serious preparations for retirement?" 45 percent indicated they were over 50 years of age. If we add the 40 to 50 year group to that number, 80 percent were over 40 years of age before they began making serious preparations for their latter years. That alone is a major hurdle to having a meaningful retirement.

In response to the question "What is the hardest challenge you face in retirement?" 32 percent indicated "limited income," and 27 percent stated "poor health." Some respondents did not list any challenge. However, if we add the two previously stated challenges together, 59 percent reported that the major challenges they faced in retirement are in areas in which an early start could make a major difference in their rest-of-life years.

I'm not attempting to indicate that the factors are totally solvable by an early start. What I *am* trying to say as strongly as possible is that an early start will have a significant impact on the quality of life during retirement years in these two areas. Admittedly, some physical issues are genetic and not the result of poor health habits. And some financial issues will be beyond our control. But by starting *now*, you'll be much better prepared for that period of your life.

To give you the main message in preparation for a meaningful life, let me pass on to you the heart and core of what many authors and retirement books say over and over. What every one of us hopes to do is live the rest-of-life portion of our time on earth in a meaningful, happy, and healthy way. We want that portion of our lives to be fulfilling and rewarding. So do not wait for that special moment to come to start making arrangements for your rest-of-life years to be what you dream them to be.

We should be able to live full lives until God calls us home. There are adjustments to be made, since our bodies change and we can no longer do what we have done for years. We will need to slow our pace and decrease our physical activity. There are also mental and emotional adjustments to make. Trust me, I've gone through them, and they can be made. But we no longer need to go to the "old folks home" or live an "an old folks life." Frankly, I plan to live—I mean really live as long as God will let me.

I have discovered that life does not end with the retirement ceremony. When that moment comes, we can restructure our lives and go on enjoying life. Yes, again, please keep in mind the adjustments that will need to be made.

I had trouble for a while understanding my body. Many times when I said, "I can do that," my body said, "I don't think so." So I learned to adjust rather than pay dearly in soreness or injury.

If we don't have a "stash of cash," and most of us don't, we can learn to get by on less. And remember, there is no stigma in working full or part time. Most authors on retirement agree that some work actually helps retirees achieve a purposeful life, while it helps keep us in shape financially. Some day we may have to shut our motors off and put everything in park, but until that sad day we can live healthy, happy, meaningful lives.

So, give serious attention to the *now* period in your life, and you'll be better prepared for the yet-to-come period. In order to keep your daydreams for retirement from turning into nightmares, you must start preparing *now!*

7
PREPARE YOUR BODY

It's amazing what we do to our bodies when we're young. We treat them as though they are indestructible and then complain when they begin to break down. If we treated our bodies the way we treat a new automobile (if we had the option of buying one), we could get more pleasant mileage from them.

In the old days, when we bought a new car, we broke it in carefully. We drove slowly for the first 500 miles and gradually built up speed to the break-in mileage of 3,000. We changed the oil at 1,000 miles, and we carefully monitored the thermostat. We prepared the car for extended service. As a result, that automobile gave mostly trouble-free travel for many, many miles.

Things have changed with new technology. We no longer have that break-in period when we drive more slowly and change the oil early. However, if we expect to receive good performance from a new car, we must still take good care of it, including changing the oil and servicing the chassis every 3,000 or 4,000 miles. We must be sure to use the correct fuel. Not all cars perform well on regular gas. And there are other points of which we are well aware.

We understand this procedure in which cars are concerned. We need to also understand this principle in which our bodies are concerned. When we take good care of our bodies (except for genetic problems), they will serve us well for many years. And even some genetic issues are improved by good physical treatment. Abuse our bodies, and like a poorly cared-for auto, they will cause us a lot of trouble. Those of you who are not yet already retired are in the "body break-in" period of life. The younger you are, the greater your opportunity is to prepare physically for a meaningful rest of life.

Let there be no mistake—the condition of our physical bodies will be a major factor in how much we're able to enjoy the retirement phase of our lives. Two major issues stood out in response to our questionnaire concerning the hardest challenges faced during retirement. The most frequent response (32 percent) listed limited income. A close second (27 percent) was poor health. I will focus in another chapter on preparations to keep limited income from being a problem. For now, the issue is poor health. Is there anything that can be done about this? In many situations the answer is yes.

I have no hesitation in stating that the pleasure you enjoy in retirement will be in close ratio to your health. You want to enjoy those after years of your life, so you must do something about it now. The longer you wait to start a healthy regimen, the greater price you will pay in health problems later on. *It's never too early to take care of your physical body.*

Start by Eating Right

I'm not a dietician, but there are some facts so basic that anyone can take advantage of them. There is no question that our bodies become what we eat. Eat an unhealthful diet, and you'll develop an unhealthy body. Then, when you reach your golden years, your body will give out on you.

I understand this principle very well. My father worked hard all his life. He was never overweight because he worked off any excess fat. Still, he died of a major heart attack. Dad's diet was awful. He ate everything fried in grease. I'm talking about the grease made from hog fat—lard. And I used to watch him eat the fat from a piece of beef as if it were candy. He ate very few vegetables and fruits. If Dad had ever had his cholesterol checked, I'm sure it would have been out of sight. In those days they were not aware of the health ramifications.

While Dad was working, he was able to keep his body going. He walked miles, including climbing hundreds of steps each day as he worked many long hours. Just two years after retiring from that hard labor, his body gave out on him. I believe that if my father had eaten more healthfully, he could have lived many more years and enjoyed being free from the 70- to 80-hour weeks he worked for so many years. My mother, who watched what she ate, is 100 and going strong. While genetics is a big factor, diet is a major contributor to our long-range health.

I certainly understand the dilemma pastors face. We are invited to multiple functions throughout each year in which food is the main feature. It's an occupational hazard. We have no control over the menu. So how do we eat healthfully without offending our host who is so excited about showing off his or her culinary skills? The first thing that comes to mind is to eat smaller portions—less than we would normally eat. Second, focus on menu servings that are compatible with good health.

I remember Christmas seasons when I was invited to multiple Sunday School class parties. I enjoyed being with our people, so I tried to attend as many of those as possible. During one Christmas season I was invited to four class parties on the same evening. That could be a quadruple disaster! However, I made it by spending 10 to 15 minutes at each party and eating very carefully. When I explained my evening schedule, every host understood and appreciated my dilemma. A simple explanation can relieve a lot of pressure.

I've already admitted that I'm not a dietician, so I won't attempt to tell you what to eat or not to eat. An abundance of information is available on that subject. One excellent resource is www.mypyramid.gov, sponsored by the U.S. Department of Agriculture. I will say that it's universally accepted that eating less fatty and sugar-filled foods will dramatically enhance your health outlook.

Watch Your Weight

I know we don't want to discuss or hear talk about our weight. However, if you're going to have a meaningful retirement, you need to give serious attention to this issue. The weight factor is closely related to eating right, but there's more to the problem than just eating.

My wife, Joyce, and I are privileged to speak for pastors' and spouses' conferences literally around the world. We work with an average of at least 1,000 to 1,500 couples each year. It's deeply disturbing to watch seriously obese servants of God overloading their plates when we know this will only add to an already obvious major problem. It's a given that if we don't take control of this area of our lives early, we will not be in control in retirement. And by the time we get to that point in our lives, our hearts will suffer, healthy knees may be gone, and countless other ailments will detract from the multitude of pleasures we should be able to enjoy.

Some authorities report that one-third of American

adults are significantly overweight. From what Joyce and I have observed, close to one-half of all ministers and spouses fall into that category.

In spite of the evidence to the contrary, many Americans refuse to recognize that we are basically obese people. The multiplication of fast-food outlets makes it easy to be overweight. The constant bombardment with slick television spots causes our taste buds to desire the flavor of this unhealthy food. And we Americans have been raised to think that we should have anything our body craves, so we refuse to change our eating habits; as we continue getting fatter, we increase the number of health problems we all face.

Many try to hide behind the low-fat or low-carb label. Remember, just because it has that label does not mean it is good for you.

Some try to hide behind the idea that a little middle-weight gain is inevitable. Some even believe that as long as cholesterol and blood pressure are under control, there is nothing to worry about. Nonsense! Even moderate obesity slows you down in numerous ways and contributes to some nasty health problems.

I have worked hard to keep my weight near where it should be. However, on a recent checkup my blood sugar was showing an alarming increase. My doctor said, "You can lose 10 pounds or go on medication." I chose to lose the weight. Now I watch more carefully than ever what I eat, I get more exercise, and I'm still off medication. It was my choice. I chose to take charge of my health rather than let it take charge of me.

So can you.

It will help everyone's future rest-of-life, if he or she stops denying that being overweight really is harmful to health and longevity.

So, will you get a life or get sick as you approach your retirement years? It really is *a choice you make before you get there.* You will discover a close relationship between your health and your happiness. So start right now investing in healthy eating habits so you'll be able to enjoy a happy retirement.

Get Plenty of Exercise

Wise is the person who follows a regular regimen of physical exercise. It is a well-established fact that the earlier you start and the longer you pursue physical exercise, the better you'll be able to control the condition of your body. Also, it's a given that the earlier you start, the stronger your foundation for physical well-being will be established. Please understand that if you wait until retirement is in sight, you will have really hindered yourself.

Exercise does more than develop muscles. While the authors are speaking to people who are already retired or who are approaching retirement years, the principle given by Cullinane and Fitzgerald in their book *The New Retirement* applies to everyone. They state that healthiness equals happiness and go on to explain:

> Sure, you feel better when you're well, but it's the physical act of exercise that brings about a shift in mood. A psychological bonanza of more pleasurable

feelings results from just a short investment of time. In one study, men and women, average age 53, completed surveys before, during, and after a 15-minute walk. Everyone reported a more positive affect (feelings or emotions) and greater energy, both during and after the walk, and felt greater calmness and relaxation 15 minutes after completing the walk.[1]

According to Cullinane and Fitzgerald, exercise helps not only our bodies but our emotions as well. And it also implies that the better health you maintain for yourself, the better health your spouse will maintain too.

I could give you a list of physical exercises that will enhance your health now and later. Some have the option of gyms or other workout facilities. Others get involved in sports activities that require extensive physical activity. A plethora of games will meet this need.

Even without access to a gym or to playing games, anyone can walk or ride a bike. As mentioned earlier, Joyce and I usually walk two miles a day. And by the way, we have found that those two miles, whether outdoors or at the mall, are a great time to communicate and connect with each other.

Unless you're limited by a physical handicap, do something right now to strengthen the physical foundation upon which you'll build your retirement years. In the same way that it's never too early to plan financially for retirement, it's also never too early to plan physically for those years.

Do your future self a favor. Start now to get in shape. If you've already started, congratulations! Just stay with the program, and help yourself to a meaningful retirement.

8
START SAVING
NOW

It's never too early to start some financial program to insure that in your retirement years your monetary needs will be met. In response to the survey question "What is the hardest challenge you face in retirement?" 32 percent indicated limited income. This major issue was present despite the fact that 99 percent were covered by Social Security and 96 percent were receiving a denominational pension of some kind.

The 32 percent figure is even more enlightening considering the fact that 53 percent of the responders had a 403(b) or tax-sheltered annuity account and 35 percent had an individual retirement account. With 99 percent in Social Security and a combined 88 percent in some retirement program, the obvious question is "What's the problem?" The answer is simple: *They did not start saving early enough.* A combined 80 percent were over 40 years of age before starting to make serious preparation for retirement. It's never too early to start. However, 40 years is a late age to begin saving.

As you read this, whatever your age is, *start now!* While you may be getting a late start, it's truly better late than never. Take it from a person whose serious plans started after age 40—it's uphill from that point. However, I'm just grateful I started then.

One respondent said that if a person can save only $5.00 per month, $5.00 is better than nothing. Take a good look at the following chart prepared by the Pensions and Benefits Office of the Church of the Nazarene. It emphasizes the importance of beginning a savings plan early:

$2,000

is more than

$12,000

? ? ?

The High Cost of Waiting

Starts Investing at Age 21		Starts Investing at Age 38
67	Age at Retirement	67
7%	Rate of Return	7%
$400	Yearly Contribution	$400
5	Years Contributing	30
$2,000	Total Amount Contributed	$12,000
$39,437	Value at Age 67	$37,784

Want Proof?

The High Cost of Waiting

Start Saving at Age 21			Start Saving at Age 38		
Age	Contribution	Value	Age	Contribution	Value
21	400	400	21	0	0
22	400	828	22	0	0
23	400	1,286	23	0	0
24	400	1,776	24	0	0
25	400	2,300	25	0	0
26	0	2,461	26	0	0
27	0	2,634	27	0	0
28	0	2,818	28	0	0
29	0	3,015	29	0	0
30	0	3,226	30	0	0
31	0	3,452	31	0	0
32	0	3,694	32	0	0
33	0	3,952	33	0	0

34	0	4,229	34	0	0
35	0	4,525	35	0	0
36	0	4,842	36	0	0
37	0	5,181	37	0	0
38	0	5,543	38	400	400
39	0	5,931	39	400	828
40	0	6,347	40	400	1,286
41	0	6,791	41	400	1,776
42	0	7,266	42	400	2,300
43	0	7,775	43	400	2,462
44	0	8,319	44	400	2,861
45	0	8,901	45	400	4,104
46	0	9,525	46	400	4,791
47	0	10,191	47	400	5,527
48	0	10,905	48	400	6,313
49	0	11,668	49	400	7,155
50	0	12,485	50	400	8,056
51	0	13,359	51	400	9,020
52	0	14,294	52	400	10,052
53	0	15,294	53	400	11,155
54	0	16,365	54	400	12,336
55	0	18,510	55	400	13,600
56	0	18,736	56	400	14,952
57	0	20,048	57	400	16,398
58	0	21,451	58	400	17,946
59	0	22,953	59	400	19,602
60	0	24,559	60	400	21,374
61	0	26,278	61	400	23,271
62	0	28,118	62	400	25,300
63	0	30,086	63	400	27,471
64	0	32,192	64	400	29,794
65	0	34,446	65	400	32,279
66	0	36,857	66	400	34,939
67	0	39,437	67	400	37,784

These are compound interest illustrations only, not accumulation guarantees.

These charts are dramatic demonstrations of how money multiplies over time. Imagine how much the 21-year-old would have had at retirement if he or she had continued the savings program.

How Much Is Needed?

One question that gets a variety of responses is "How much do I need so that I will be financially secure at retirement time?" The answer depends upon who is responding. Those in the business of selling or providing retirement programs usually call for a greater amount than those who are not in the business.

One rule of thumb is 60 to 80 percent of your current income will be needed. However, I can point to many retired ministers who are enjoying life on less. It may depend upon the level of life you want to have.

It is a given that if you still have children at home or in college, you will need more than those who do not. Also, it is a given that if you choose to live in the resort areas of Florida, Arizona, and similar places, you will need more. However, if you plan to downsize your house and live in a reasonably priced area, you will be surprised at how happy you can be on less than 60 to 80 percent. The real answer to how much you need will depend on what you decide after considering your retirement plans.

This is the way Steve Vernon responded to the question, "How much do I need to retire?"

Now that I'm in my third quarter of life, I've been giving this question some serious thought. I've come to realize that my old ways of thinking about retirement are out of touch with the new realities of working and living in our later years. We baby boomers need a new model of living the rest of our lives—a model for the twenty-first century.[1]

So, basically whether you need 60 to 80 percent or less (or more) depends on the lifestyle you choose and where you decide to live.

In making preparations so you won't experience misery, you need to plan well enough so that your income will exceed expenses. In this regard as you approach retirement, and certainly by the age of 50 to 60, take a sheet of paper and list all the monthly income you anticipate having when you retire. On another sheet, list all the expenses you expect to encounter. Add each list and compare them. By doing this at that age, you'll know if you need to increase your retirement deposits in order to attain the lifestyle you desire. If you cannot increase your savings, you'll need to reconsider your plans for retirement.

You may need to plan for less travel. And you may need to decide that rather than living in a place where the weather is nice but the cost of living is much higher, you should plan to live in a less exotic area. Also, rather than maintaining a three-bedroom home, you may want to consider a smaller apartment.

If your projected income does not exceed your projected expenses, you need to downsize your retirement expectations. Don't wait until you retire to discover your retirement dreams have become nightmares. By looking ahead and planning carefully, you'll find your retirement dreams can come true.

Another chart prepared by the Nazarene Pensions and Benefits Office offers some insight into how much money is needed.

How Long Will It Last?

The chart shows how long $100,000 will last given various rates of return with an assumed annual 4 percent increase in withdrawal amount, adjusted for inflation.

Withdrawals Starting At*	Years Money Will Last Invested at the Following Yields				
	4%	6%	8%	10%	12%
$2,000	50	151	FOREVER		
$6,000	17	20	25	43	FOREVER
$10,000	10	11	12	14	17
$14,000	7	8	8	9	10

*Assumes single withdrawal at first of year, increasing each year by 4 percent to cover inflation.

According to this chart, if you can accumulate $100,000 and then invest it at 8 percent, you can withdraw $6,000 per year or $500 per month for 25 years before exhausting these funds. This chart will help you plan for future financial needs. If, like 99 percent of the survey responders, you're covered by Social Security and you receive a denomination-al pension, as 96 percent do, you'll have a monthly income in the neighborhood of $2,000. This amount will vary de-pending upon your years of contribution to Social Security and years of service in ministry.

While many speculate about the survival of Social Security, most financial people believe there will always be something there. According to Ralph Warner, unless some major disaster prevents it, Social Security benefits will continue to be paid well into the middle of the century.[2]

One major unknown in looking to the rest-of-life experience is the issue of health. As stated in chapter 6, while you can prepare for a healthier retirement, you can be absolutely sure some health problems will arise. Again, the survey pointed out that 27 percent of retirees have serious health issues. It is also helpful to notice that 39 percent have minor health problems. That means that 66 percent of retirees face medical difficulties of some nature. You should anticipate some health expenses in your retirement.

I hope you're covered by Medicare or Medicaid. However, this is only a starting point for help with medical expenses. If possible, maintain some form of second-level coverage through an insurance company. Still, no one gets a free health coverage ride, and the respondents to the survey express concern. In the survey 83 percent had insurance coverage, while 11 percent said, "Yes—but I worry that I'll not be able to continue affording the premiums." So this financial need is a given. What's unpredictable is the costs that will be there.

What About Work?

Many people approach retirement with the idea that their working days are over. When they enter these golden years and discover they don't have enough gold and need to mine some more, they're disillusioned, and some become depressed. Let me say as strongly as possible—there's nothing wrong with continuing some level of work following retirement.

I've now been retired nine years. I still stay active in ministry as opportunities become available. Sometimes the schedule gets crowded, but as a retiree, I have the option of doing only what I want to do when I want to.

Some may feel a bit of stigma because they need to work. There's absolutely no reason for anyone to feel that way. Listen to what Steve Vernon writes in his book *Live Long and Prosper:* "As will be demonstrated again and again, money has relatively little to do with successful aging. . . . As you get older you need people, not dollars and cents."[3]

Employment in retirement seems to be a major issue for many "yet to retire" ministers. I have never understood the stigma that some people in ministry feel about the need to take on secular work to have enough money to provide physical needs. As a young pastor, I had to supplement my salary to have the financial strength I needed. I was not embarrassed to work outside the church. I used these occasions as opportunities to make contact for the Kingdom. So it has been easy for me to work in retirement.

I have enough retirement funds so that my wife and I could scale back on activities, downsize our home, and get by. But why? I still love the privilege of interacting with people. Even as I write these lines, I am in my office as chaplain of a new theme park that is scheduled to open in a few weeks. The financial help will be nice, but at the age of 75, getting to interact with the hundreds of young people who will work here brings great joy to my heart. Not only am I not embarrassed by my work, but I am excited about it.

You may not have the option of a theme park, but you can do something that will allow you to stay in contact with people. That's what should give you hope and happiness, not having enough money so that you don't have to work.

The good life comes from identifying and applying the strengths and gifts God has entrusted to us. The greatest potential any of us have is making the most of our signature strengths.

Many people, as Steve Vernon observes, find themselves "caught in a trap regarding the pleasurable life." Before retirement they spend their money to maintain a certain lifestyle but fail to save for the future. Then to make matters worse they overestimate the money they need to retire because they include the expense of continuing that special lifestyle—a lifestyle lacking "true satisfaction."[4]

While we want enough money to meet our needs, it's not money that provides a meaningful retirement. *What produces a meaningful ministerial retirement is our attitude toward God's call, God's people, and God's provision.*

So *start now!* Save all you can. Get your financial house in order. I'm not a financial planner, but the world is full of professionals who want to help you, and you might want to find one. However, some things are basic and must be included in your financial program to secure your future happiness.

- Pay off all credit cards and eliminate those high interest rates.

- While many retirement planners recommend that you pay off your home mortgage, that may not be the best approach for ministers. Tax laws are structured so that withdrawals for housing expenses can be made from church retirement plans and are not subject to taxes. In the early days of retirement, this can make a significant difference in your tax liability. If your house is paid off, you can withdraw only for upkeep and maintenance. If a mortgage still exists, you can withdraw the payment without liability.

- Participate in your denomination's recommended retirement savings program. Deposit something into this account on a regular basis. Even small amounts can become significant if started early. Such programs are designed to comply with all tax laws and usually charge little or no fees. The fee-free structure can be a major savings to you.

Preparing financially for retirement is a major step in enjoying the rest-of-life years. No one can tell you just how much you will need; however, all people need money. No one lives free from financial responsibility. The better prepared you are, the less pressure you will feel. The less pressure you feel, the more pleasure you'll have in your golden years.

In concluding this chapter, I want to share something from an excellent article in the March 17, 2006, *USA Today* newspaper. The writer, John Waggoner, said he asked retirement experts to find the five biggest mistakes people made when entering retirement. Here is the resulting list:

- Not saving enough. . . .
- Not having an emergency fund. . . .
- Not diversifying. . . .
- Not counting health care costs. . . .
- Not getting all the paperwork done. . . .[5]

Retirement planning isn't easy, but if you avoid these five mistakes, your biggest worry might be finding the right velvet painting for your living room.

Want a meaningful retirement? *Start now!*

9
GET READY INTERNALLY

I have already quoted Lee Iacocca, but his statement is worth another look. "Everybody says you've got to get ready financially. No, No! You've got to get ready psychologically."

It is critical that you prepare yourself for that moment when you are no longer "the pastor" or worship leader or whatever ministerial role you filled or may still be filling. When your day of retirement comes, you may find yourself asking the question "Who am I?" And if you are like most retirees, it will take a while to find a suitable answer.

The loss of our identities can be a more serious hill to climb than being in good health or having a strong financial plan. Take it from one who has been there. Frankly, no longer being Pastor Williams left me with an empty feeling inside.

I realized, though, that I could still be involved in ministry, and I have been blessed to do that. I'm grateful for the opportunities that came. But in all honesty, there was a huge void in my emotions. I still share what H. B. London Jr. wrote in his book *They Call Me Pastor*:

> The first time someone called me pastor, it seemed strange. I not only felt too young to carry that title, but I also didn't feel worthy or ready for the responsibilities that accompanied that God-ordained office (see Eph. 4:11). But I grew to love that title and to this day respond to it with joy. It made me feel special when they called me pastor.
>
> Pastor,
>
> > . . . thanks for the sermon.
> >
> > . . . I need to talk with you.
> >
> > . . . my mom just died.
> >
> > . . . we are going to have a baby.
> >
> > . . . God seems to be directing us to another church.

. . . I believe God has called me into the ministry. How can *I know for sure?*

. . . the X-rays do not look good. Could you pray with me?

. . . we will be moving to the East Coast next week. We will miss you.

. . . when do you think you'll have time to get a haircut?

. . . I'm gay . . . what should I do?

. . . we are praying for you.

. . . my wife just left me.

. . . our daughter is pregnant.

. . . thanks for being there when I needed you.

The list is endless, but you know what I mean and how it feels.[1]

I was not prepared, and as I admitted previously, I went into some depression. I had not looked ahead to the day I would no longer be on the frontline of ministry. I am one of those who thought the status quo would go on forever. Retirement was for old people, and I would never get there. But I did. I desperately needed to know, "Who am I? What does God want from me?"

It took several months for me to understand that all He wanted was for me to continue to love Him, His people, and to serve in whatever capacity He provided for me. After years of being on the frontlines of ministry, I was finally able to accept a backup role, and my depression came to an end.

I confess there are still times when the old warhorse in

me wants to go back to the frontlines. As I mentioned earlier, on many occasions my heart says, "I can do that," but my body replies, "I don't think so!"

This is an adjustment each one of us must make. It is interesting that while every retirement book speaks strongly to financial and health preparations, they say little about psychological and emotional preparations. Perhaps this is because they are writing to people in secular employment. These folks may not always get so emotionally attached to their work as those of us in ministry do.

I have admitted I had a real struggle "letting go" of pastoral ministry. I was addicted to it and thought it would continue forever. It didn't. So I had to do some real internal work on myself. I soon realized God had other plans for me. I believed I had been a good pastor, but now I could pursue another less-demanding area of ministry.

In a way, there came a new releasing of my life to God. He is not bound to using you or me in only one area. He has other things for us to do. And quite frankly, I am having as much fun now as I did when pastoring. Plus, now when I'm tired or want to play golf, fish, or travel, I don't have to think twice about what anyone thinks. This is truly a great life! So as you approach retirement, cast out of your mind the idea of totally removing yourself from ministry.

Again, the retired ministers' survey helps us: 52 percent are involved in ongoing ministry of some kind; 54 percent have found new possibilities for community involvement. After reading the subjective responses, I am confident that those retirees who stay active to some degree enjoy life much more than those who totally withdraw. In view of that, you will help yourself by looking past total retirement to the more satisfying and meaningful position of *retired but available.*

Live a Regretless Life

Is it possible to live a life without regrets? Absolutely! We may not always attain the goals with which we entered ministry or ascend the heights of other ministerial friends and acquaintances. However, if we give the call everything we have and take advantage of the opportunities God gives us, we have every reason to retire with our heads held high.

I have many friends who will join me in testifying to this fact. You never saw their names in bold print on anything, but when you get to heaven you'll realize they were part of a committed army that fought the good fight of faith. They retired and live without regrets.

The time before we retire is the time to lay the groundwork for a regretless life. Art Linkletter and Mark Victor Hansen give great insights about how to accomplish this in their book *How to Make the Rest of Your Life the Best of Your Life:*

> Here's the difficult part: If you've reached 50, 55 or 60 with a negative outlook on life, a cargo of regret on your shoulders, or no sense of humor, how do you develop positive thinking habits? Like most of us, you know from years of experience that it's very difficult to change the habits of years or decades. So how do you live without regret?

Like all things . . . you make a choice. That choice has four aspects to it:

1. *Close the book of past pains. . . .*
2. *Set goals for the future. . . .*
3. *Do what you've always wanted to do. . . .*
4. *Affirm your new view every day.*[2]

So there you have it. Now, prepare yourself internally for the day when you enter the rest of your life. Even with the best of preparations, you may very well have some struggling moments as I did. I admit, as I did earlier, that I struggled with the transition; however, as He does in every phase of our lives, the Father helped me, and you can be sure He will help you as well. All of those wonderful promises we have shared with others apply to us as well—promises like

Prov. 3:5-6

Isa. 30:19-21

Jer. 29:11

1 John 3:21

Rom. 8:28

John 14:13-14

So if these wonderful promises are good for our people who sit in our pews, aren't they also good for those of us who stand in the pulpit? I hear your answer—a resounding "Of course they are!" If they are good for anyone, they are surely good for those of us who have given our lives to His kingdom work.

In that positive attitude of faith I urge you to get ready for the rest of your life and plan to enjoy a meaningful ministerial retirement.

EPILOGUE

While working on these lines, I spent many hours reading in my favorite chair. This isn't just any old chair. It's *the chair* I bought in 1953 at Sears & Roebuck in Kansas City for $39.95 when I started studying at seminary. As any seminarian will tell you, those studies require a ton of reading. So it is absolutely essential to have a comfortable location in which to study.

My chair is now well over 50 years old and has been dragged all over the country. It has been eaten in and spilled on, and who knows what else has happened in it. Along the way that chair has been re-covered several times—once in a ghoulish blue vinyl. That cover was so ugly that my first wife, Bettye, banned the chair from the house.

Most people would probably have thrown it away, but I became emotionally attached to it. I met with my Heavenly Father many, many times in that chair, and hundreds of sermons were born during those times. There was just something special about the comfortable embrace of that chair, so I kept it around.

The chair finally ended up in a dusty corner of the attic over the garage in our house. Bettye insisted on taking it there when the ugly blue vinyl began to crack and didn't match anything in our house. I couldn't blame her.

Two years after Bettye's untimely death, God brought Joyce into my life. Shortly after we were married, I took her up into the attic and showed her some old keepsakes. Then I went on to explain why I continued to hold onto them. When I told her that most of my sermons had been born in that chair, her mind went to work.

While I was on a hunting trip, she secretly had the chair removed from the attic, re-covered, and restored, making it look as good as new. Since I didn't frequent the attic, I never missed the chair.

What a day it was when Joyce reunited me with *the chair* on the following Father's Day! I cannot tell you how happy I was with the return of my old friend. Tears of joy filled our eyes as I sank into the familiar comfort of its warm embrace.

Now, what has an old chair got to do with retirement? If we assume there's not a message here, we miss the wonderful transformation of a once new young chair to an experienced, beautiful, and very usable old chair. No, not many sermons come from it anymore, but it's there in my special corner where I meet with the Lord every morning.

It's also significant that the chair is no longer confined to a dusty attic corner or wasting away in a landfill. It could have been and would have been if adjustments had not been made to keep it usable. I confess, it doesn't look the same as it did in 1953, but it still has great value to its owner.

Some of you who read these lines are still in the seminary years of your life, with a long and great future before you. Others are in the blue vinyl years, and some of you may feel you've been abandoned in a dark, dusty attic corner.

The message of the chair is that your Owner is attached to you, and He will never, ever throw you away. You are still useful to Him and the Kingdom regardless of your phase in life.

Hang on! Never lose sight of what He who called you into ministry has in mind for you. If you are in the attic, get out! Determine to do something that will be useful for the Kingdom. The rest of you must look forward to always retaining your value. Remember Jer. 29:11: "'I know the plans I have for you,' declares the LORD, 'plans to prosper you and not to harm you, plans to give you hope and a future.'"

NOTES

Introduction

1. Julia Burton-Jones, online article, "Retirement: A Second Vocation" (September 2003), © copyright The Jubilee Centre, 2003 <http://www.jubilee-centre.org/online_documents/RetirementASecondVocation.htm>.

2. Ibid.

3. Ibid.

4. Muriel Larson, online article, "Retirement Without Trauma," in *Retirement with a Purpose*, monthly e-zine. Copyright © 2007 Retirement with a Purpose, a ministry of Campus Crusade for Christ <http://retirementwithapurpose.com/opportunity/mlretirenotrauma.html>.

5. Ibid.

6. Mark Victor Hansen and Art Linkletter, *How to Make the Rest of Your Life the Best of Your Life* (Nashville: Thomas Nelson, 2006), 210.

Chapter 1

1. Jan Cullinane and Cathy Fitzgerald, *The New Retirement: The Ultimate Guide to the Rest of Your Life* (Emmaus, Pa.: Rodale Books, 2004), 4.

2. Wes Tracy, *Younger than I Used to Be* (Kansas City: Beacon Hill Press of Kansas City, 2006), 121-22.

3. Cullinane and Fitzgerald, *New Retirement*, 15.

4. Tracy, *Younger than I Used to Be*, 20.

Chapter 2

1. Got Questions Ministries, "What Is the Christian View of Retirement?" *GotQuestions.org*, http://www.gotquestions.org/retirement-Christian.html (accessed May 14, 2007).

2. Ibid.

3. Richard G. Capen Jr., *Finish Strong* (Grand Rapids: Zondervan, 1998), 7.

4. Ibid., 143.

5. Ibid., 147.

6. Dave Thomas, *Dave Says . . . Well Done!* (Grand Rapids: Zondervan, 1994), 220.

7. Anthony Bradley, "See, Some Christians Really Don't Retire," *World on the Web*, http://anthonybradley.worldmagblog.com/anthonybradley/archives/2004_04.html (accessed May 14, 2007).

Chapter 3

1. Dwight Hervey Small, *When Christians Retire: Finding New Purpose in Your Bonus Years* (Kansas City: Beacon Hill Press of Kansas City, 2000), 6.

2. Ibid., 8-9.

3. Ibid.

4. Tracy, *Younger than I Used to Be*, 127.

5. Ibid.

6. Ibid., 129.

7. Bill Tammeus, "Ministry for Life," *Kansas City Star* (November 5, 2005).

8. Ibid.

9. Ibid.

10. Quoted in Cullinane and Fitzgerald, *New Retirement*, 93.

11. Stan Hinden, *How to Retire Happy: The 12 Most Important Decisions You Must Make Before You Retire* (New York: McGraw-Hill, 2006), 10.

12. Ibid., 10-11.

13. Ibid.

14. Ibid., 12.

15. Ralph Warner, *Get a Life: You Don't Need a Million to Retire Well*, 5th ed. (Berkeley, Calif.: NOLO, 2004), 54.

16. Ibid., 57.

Chapter 4

1. Warner, *Get a Life*, 150.

2. Charles R. Swindoll, *Man to Man* (Grand Rapids: Zondervan, 1996), 63-64; emphasis added.

3. Ron Mehl, *Surprise Endings: Ten Good Things About Bad Things* (Sisters, Oreg.: Questar Publishers, 1993), 14.

4. Small, *When Christians Retire*, 13.

5. Ibid., 101.

6. Cullinane and Fitzgerald, *New Retirement*, 29.

7. Hansen and Linkletter, *How to Make the Rest of Your Life the Best of Your Life*, 9-10.

8. Hinden, *How to Retire Happy*, 218-20.

9. Capen, *Finish Strong*, 40.

Chapter 6

1. Steve Vernon, *Live Long and Prosper: Invest in Your Happiness, Health and Wealth for Retirement and Beyond* (Hoboken, N.J.: John Wiley and Sons, 2005), 11-12.

2. Cullinane and Fitzgerald, *New Retirement*, 3.

Chapter 7

1. Cullinane and Fitzgerald, *New Retirement*, 19-20.

Chapter 8

1. Vernon, *Live Long and Prosper*, 1-2.

2. Warner, *Get a Life*, 240-41.

3. Vernon, *Live Long and Prosper*, 48.

4. Ibid., 49-50.

5. John Waggoner, "How to Avoid Ruining Retirement: Avoid These Five Common Pitfalls to Help Insure a Bright Future," *USA Today*, 17 (March 2006).

Chapter 9

1. H. B. London Jr., *They Call Me Pastor* (Ventura, Calif.: Regal Books, 2000), 11. Used by permission.

2. Hansen and Linkletter, *How to Make the Rest of Your Life the Best of Your Life*, 221-23.